DUBLIN

ENCOUNTER

FIONN DAVENPORT
ODA O'CARROLL

Dublin Encounter

Published by Lonely Planet Publications Pty Ltd
ABN 36 005 607 983

Australia	Head Office, Locked Bag 1, Footscray, Vic 3011
	☎ 03 8379 8000 fax 03 8379 8111
	talk2us@lonelyplanet.com.au
USA	150 Linden St, Oakland, CA 94607
	☎ 510 893 8555
	toll free 800 275 8555
	fax 510 893 8572
	info@lonelyplanet.com
UK	72–82 Rosebery Ave, Clerkenwell, London EC1R 4RW
	☎ 020 7841 9000 fax 020 7841 9001
	go@lonelyplanet.co.uk

This title was commissioned in Lonely Planet's London office and produced by: **Commissioning Editors** Fiona Buchan, Janine Eberle **Coordinating Editors** Michael Day, Justin Flynn, Emma Gilmour **Coordinating Cartographers** Dan Fennessy, Erin McManus, Mandy Sierp, Andrew Smith, Herman So, Simon Tillema **Layout Designer** Gary Newman **Managing Editors** Imogen Bannister, Melanie Dankel, Katie Lynch **Managing Cartographer** Mark Griffiths **Cover Designer** James Hardy **Project Manager** Eoin Dunlevy **Series Designers** Nic Lehman, Wendy Wright **Thanks to** Yvonne Byron, Sally Darmody, Bruce Evans, Kate Evans, Jennifer Garrett, Michelle Glynn, Laura Jane, Katie Lynch, Kate McDonald, Cahal McGroarty, Paul Piaia, Stephanie Pearson, Lauren Rollheiser, Wibowo Rusli, Vivek Wagle, Celia Wood, Evelyn Yee

ISBN 978 1 74059 829 3

Printed through Colorcraft Ltd, Hong Kong.
Printed in China

Acknowledgement Dublin Transit Map © Iarnród éireann 2006

HOW TO USE THIS BOOK

Colour-Coding & Maps

Colour-coding is used for symbols on maps and in the text that they relate to (eg all eating venues on the maps and in the text are given a green knife-and-fork symbol). Each neighbourhood also gets its own colour, and this is used down the edge of the page and throughout that neighbourhood section.

Shaded yellow areas on the maps are to denote 'areas of interest' – be that for historical significance, attractive architecture or a strip that's good for bars or restaurants. We'd encourage you to head to these areas and just start exploring!

Prices

Multiple prices listed with reviews (eg €10/5 or €10/5/20) indicate adult/child, adult/concession or adult/child/family.

Although the authors and Lonely Planet have taken all reasonable care in preparing this book, we make no warranty about the accuracy or completeness of its content and, to the maximum extent permitted, disclaim all liability arising from its use.

Send us your Feedback We love to hear from readers – your comments help make our books better. We read every word you send us, and we always guarantee that your feedback goes straight to the appropriate authors. The most useful submissions are rewarded with a free book. To send us your updates and find out about Lonely Planet events, newsletters and travel news visit our award-winning website: **www.lonelyplanet.com/contact**.

Note: We may edit, reproduce and incorporate your comments in Lonely Planet products such as guidebooks, websites and digital products, so let us know if you don't want your comments reproduced or your name acknowledged. For a copy of our privacy policy visit **www.lonelyplanet.com/feedback**.

FIONN DAVENPORT

Half Italian and a lifelong supporter of Liverpool Football Club, Fionn is the perfect Dubliner, in love with the city of his birth but one eye forever on somewhere else. He's left his city many times – for years at a stretch – but always he returns, because it's the only place on earth that treats gallows' humour as high art; why look for a straight answer when a funny one is far more satisfying?

ODA O'CARROLL

From the far reaches of midwest Ireland, Oda packed her kitbag at 17 and went to the big smoke to study Communications. She has pretty much lived there ever since. She has worked as a TV researcher, screenwriter and director, and worked on Lonely Planet's *Britain, Ireland, Dublin, France, Corsica* and *Caribbean* guides. She lives in Dublin with her husband and three daughters.

FIONN THANKS

My thanks to Oda O'Carroll, whose sterling efforts on the original manuscript may have been shifted around but was still the raw material from which this book was made.

ODA THANKS

I would like to thank Fiona in the London office; Kate, Clare, Charlotte, Katell and Orla for helping me suss out new eateries. Big shout to Mary, Brian, Sol, Shona, Ashling, Etain and Lisa for all the help and to the ever-patient Eoin and my gorgeous junior cartographers Ésa, Mella and Minnie.

Our Readers Many thanks to the travellers who wrote to us with helpful hints, useful advice and interesting anecdotes. NK Campbell, Dick Kriegmont, Lynn Rovida.

Photographs p58, p93, p132 by Fionn Davenport. All other photographs by Lonely Planet Images, and by Doug McKinlay except p12, p18, p30, p82, p116 Olivier Cirendini; p110, 121, 138, Eoin Clarke; p28, p32, p51, p119, p141 Richard Cummins; p148 Corinne Humphrey; p10, p20, p40, p76, p137 Hannah Levy; p43, p75, p78, p135 Martin Moos; p15, p16, p23, p102, p155 Jonathan Smith; p95, p114, p146 Oliver Strewe; p25 Wayne Walton; p106 Corey Wise. **Cover photograph** Kegs outside Temple Bar, Richard Cummins/Lonely Planet Images.

All images are copyright of the photographers unless otherwise indicated. Many of the images in this guide are available for licensing from **Lonely Planet Images:** www.lonelyplanetimages.com.

Céilidh (group Irish dance) at Comhaltas Ceoltó iri Éireann (p136)

CONTENTS

THIS IS DUBLIN

Busy, bustling Dublin is a million exaggerated stories that often conflict and contradict each other. No two people's experience of it is ever alike, such are the surprises in store. But don't worry: there are only a few things you need to know about Dublin. The rest is detail.

One, it's small. The city centre is bordered by two canals, north and south, and you can get anywhere on foot (or as Dubliners might say, at least anywhere that's worth going). Two, it's lively. With one of the youngest populations of any city in Europe, Dublin is alive with bars, restaurants and nightlife, and full of people who know how to live it large. Three, it's friendly. Lift a map and you'll attract a host of locals who'll show you where to go and will probably walk part of the way with you. Sit alone at a bar and before long someone will know your name and think they know someone from your town. Four, it's cosmopolitan. Gone are the days when avocados were considered exotic and olive oil was only available from chemists. With a healthy and sizeable influx of foreign nationals over the last decade, Dublin has become a proper multicultural hub, something that has given the city's arts and culinary scenes a good kick in the pants.

Oh yes, and the sights. You'll be having such a good time it'll be easy to miss the wonders of the city's many museums and galleries, or its elegant Georgian squares.

One of the best things about Dublin is that you don't have to be 'in the know' to know where to go: you'll stumble across it. If you want hip, the town is buzzing with off-beat bars and cool restaurants; if you want culture, there's a living legacy of music, art and literature; if you want to pay homage at Bono's door, well, just ask a taxi driver. Dublin is easy. As you'll soon find out.

Top left Street musician, Temple Bar (p66) **Top right** SoDa (p80) **Bottom** Moore Street Market (p114)

>HIGHLIGHTS

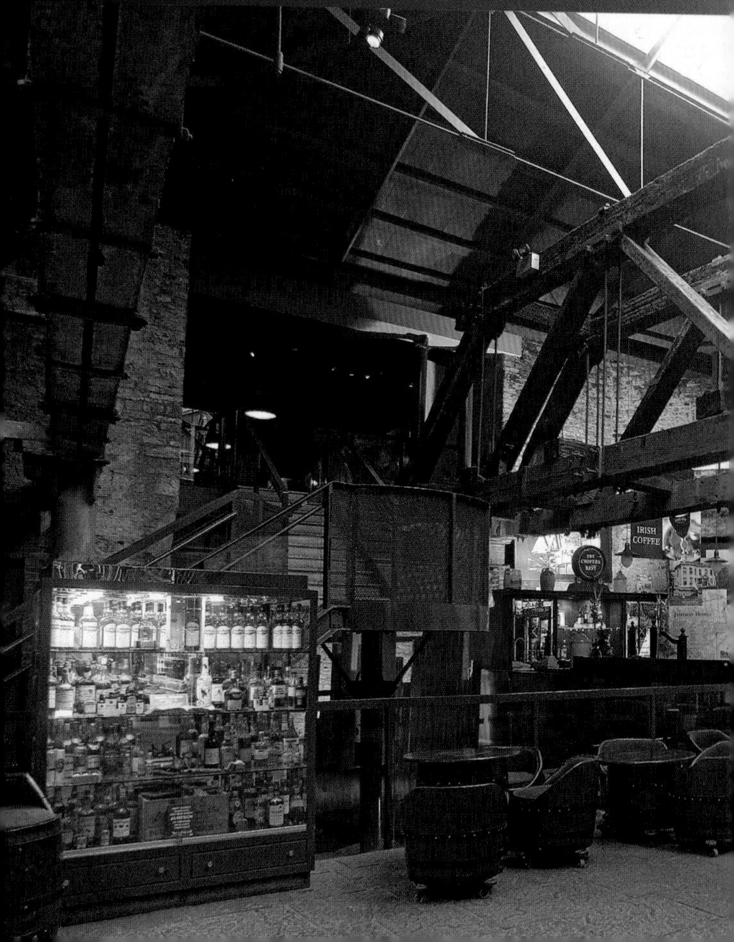

Old Jameson Distillery (p125)

> 1 TRINITY COLLEGE

A STROLL THROUGH THE LOFTY ELIZABETHAN ACADEME OF TRINITY

Entering through the Regent House archway onto Front Sq and leaving the noisy bustle of Dame St behind feels like you're stepping back in time to a more genteel era of august academia, cricket matches and Pimms parties on the lawn. There may be a debate over whether it's the city's foremost university, but there's no argument that it's by far the prettiest, the most central and easily the most evocative of Dublin's institutes of higher learning (see p40 for more information).

It's been more than 400 years in the practice, ever since Elizabeth I granted a charter to its founders in 1592 so that they may stop Irish youth from being 'infected with popery'. (One of its founders, by the way, was Archbishop Narcissus Ussher, who dated the act of Creation to 6006 BC – we thought you'd want to know.) Today the bigotry that led to its establishment has been consigned to history, but there's no escaping the scent of privilege that pervades the place, from the cobbled squares lined with handsome Victorian buildings

(most of the original structures have long since been replaced) to the carefully manicured playing fields at the back, where on summer days cricket matches are played before an appreciative audience sitting on the deck of the Pavilion Bar, drinks in hand.

Dublin's very own slice of Oxbridge aside, Trinity is home to that most Irish of treasures, the *Book of Kells*, which ironically is not Irish at all but Scottish – for it was created on the island of Iona before being transported to Kells in AD 806 so that it wouldn't fall into the hands of Viking raiders. A glimpse of it is an absolute must, but it's about as much as you'll get: its popularity and the way it is exhibited ensures that visitors are ushered past quickly and efficiently, without any time to linger and savour its beauty.

SCHOOL ON SCREEN

Trinity College has been used as a location on screen many times. Neil Jordan filmed scenes here in his 1996 film *Michael Collins*, and in the 1983 classic *Educating Rita*, starring Julie Walters and Michael Caine, Rita sits her nerve-racking end of year exams in the Exam Hall.

>2 GUINNESS STOREHOUSE

A PINT OF BLACK GOLD AT THE MOTHER OF ALL BREWERIES

More Dublin than Joyce, the Liffey and Temple Bar put together, Guinness is the very lifeblood of the city, the liquid that courses through the arteries of its streets, fuelling 1001 experiences daily. So what better place to sample a pint of the black gold than its spiritual home, where every year 450 million litres of the stuff is brewed and exported to 150 countries around the world?

Housed in an old grain storehouse opposite the original St James's Gate Brewery, this is the city's most visited tourist attraction, an all-singing, all-dancing extravaganza combining sophisticated exhibits, spectacular design and a thick, creamy head of marketing hype.

OK, so you'll make your way through the various exhibits outlining the history of the beer and the brewery, from the original charter (exhibited beneath the glass floor in the lobby) to a whole section devoted to advertising (the iconic poster and TV campaigns that have helped sell the brand worldwide). Some of the exhibits are indeed pretty fascinating, but who are we kidding? Your final destination is what this place is really all about – the top floor Gravity Bar,

where you get to drink a free glass of Guinness with a 360-degree backdrop of the city. Guinness doesn't travel well, or so everyone believes, so the one you'll have here is reputedly the best one you'll have anywhere; hundreds of thousands of personalised tests, including our own, seem to validate the theory. It's cold, beautifully bitter and oh so very black, but the key ingredient to enjoying a pint is the company of friends, so make sure you have a couple of them around when you quaff that brew.

For more on the Guinness Storehouse see p102.

G-FORCE GUINNESS

It might be an enduring favourite, but that isn't to say that Dublin's favourite pint has remained unchanged since it first bubbled into existence in 1759. Ireland's new 9000-strong Nigerian community were dismayed to taste the 'watery' 4.5% alcohol brew on sale, which they felt paled in comparison to the potent 7.5% version back home. Nigeria is Guinness' third-largest market (after Ireland and Britain), and the increased volume harks back to the 18th century when fortified beer was produced to survive the ship's long journey to Africa. Guinness duly responded to the complaint, and now the famous Dublin Guinness Foreign Extra satisfies the discerning Nigerian palate.

>3 CHESTER BEATTY LIBRARY

GETTING IN TOUCH WITH YOUR SPIRITUAL SIDE AT CHESTER BEATTY LIBRARY

Away from the hubbub of the street, beyond the ordinary distractions outside, is one of Europe's most outstanding museums, a tranquil place of beauty and reflection whose astounding collection has the power to bring serenity and peace to those who visit it. And the best bit is that relatively few people ever do!

The collection in question was gathered by New York mining magnate Sir Alfred Chester Beatty (1875–1968), whose passion for the intricately decorated manuscripts, bindings and calligraphies he found on his journeys to Egypt and the Far East resulted in his amassing more than 20,000 manuscripts, scrolls, religious books and *objets d'art,* many of which are carefully displayed over two floors.

Unlike so many other museums, which seek to wow the visitor with scale, the Chester Beatty's collection is compact and can be easily visited in no more than half an hour. But the muted ambience encourages you to slow down and savour each individual piece – or watch one of the many audiovisual displays explaining some feature or another.

Exquisite displays range from intricately designed medicine boxes and Chinese jade books, to ancient Egyptian papyri and an extraordinary collections of Korans (the best in the West).

When you're finally done with the collection, you can ponder the passage of life in the small Japanese Garden upstairs, or grab a terrific lunch in the Silk Road Café.

For details see p82.

>4 IRISH MUSEUM OF MODERN ART (IMMA)

DISTINGUISHING YOUR HIRST FROM YOUR HOCKNEY IN AN OLD SOLDIERS' HOME FOR NEW ART

Even if the thought of modern art leaves you cold, the setting of the IMMA will undoubtedly provide reason enough to visit. The country's top contemporary art gallery is spectacularly located in the former Royal Hospital Kilmainham, the city's finest surviving 17th-century building. The grounds, with their long tree-lined avenue and fountain-filled Formal Garden with views across the Liffey to Phoenix Park, make a fantastic place to stroll.

Built between 1680 and 1684, this fine building with a striking façade inspired by Les Invalides in Paris, is laid-out with a central cobbled courtyard. Inside, the light-filled museum juxtaposes the work of major established artists with that of up-and-comers. The gallery's 4000-strong collection includes works by Picasso, Miró and Vasarely, as well as more contemporary artists including Gilbert and George, Gillian Wearing and Damien Hirst. The gallery displays ever-changing shows from its own works, and hosts touring exhibitions.

Modern Irish art is always on display and Irish and international artists live and work on-site in the converted coach houses. The New Galleries, in the restored Deputy Master's House, should not be missed.

For more on the museum see p102.

> 5 ST STEPHEN'S GREEN

PLAY, STROLL OR SNOOZE IN DUBLIN'S FAVOURITE GREEN LUNG

Workers at lunch, lovers and layabouts can be found splayed about its nine manicured hectares at the merest hint of sun, content among the green lawns and fowl-filled ponds, sharing food and a laugh with each other while the sun shines.

Once upon a time, handsome St Stephen's Green was a common where public whippings, burnings and hangings took place; these days, the worst punishment is a telling off by the warden for careless cycling or for kicking a ball on the grass – with lawns like these, it's almost impossible to resist.

The fine Georgian buildings around the square date mainly from Dublin's 18th-century boom. During the 1916 Easter Rising, a band of Irish rebel forces occupied St Stephen's Green, led by the colourful Irish nationalist Countess Constance Markievicz, later the first woman elected to the Irish Parliament. Markievicz failed to take the grand Shelbourne Hotel, a popular society meeting place (although gunshots apparently disturbed the ladies at lunch, with bullets flying

through the windows), but the rebels did seize the Royal College of Surgeons building on the western side of the square. If you look closely at its columns you can still see the bullet marks.

A few doors from the Shelbourne is a small Huguenot Cemetery, established in 1693 for French Protestant refugees. The south side is home to the beautifully restored Newman House (p59) and the Byzantine-inspired Newman University Church (p60).

Statues and memorials dot the green, including those of Sir Arthur Guinness and James Joyce. Around the central fountain are busts of Countess Markievicz and a 1967 Henry Moore sculpture of WB Yeats.

Also see p61.

NO SUCH THING AS A FREE MUNCH

Dubliners U2 were conferred with Freedom of the City in a dazzling ceremony in 2000. Not shy of the odd publicity stroke, it didn't take Bono and the Edge long to invoke one of the ancient privileges of their new-found 'freedom' – the right to graze sheep on common ground within the city boundaries. It was an honour they duly carried on the lawns of St Stephen's Green, to much public amusement, with two borrowed lambs the following morning.

>6 KILMAINHAM GAOL

THE GAOL WHERE BEATS THE GRUESOME HEART OF IRISH HISTORY, IN ALL ITS DEFIANT GLORY

If you have any interest in Irish history, especially the juicy bits about resistance to English rule, you will be shaken and stirred by a visit to this infamous, eerie prison. It was the stage for many of the most tragic and heroic episodes in Ireland's recent past, and the list of its inmates reads like a who's who of Irish nationalism. Solid and sombre, its walls absorbed the barbarism of British occupation and recount them in whispers to every visitor.

After the 1916 Easter Rising, 14 of the 15 rebel executions took place at Kilmainham. James Connolly, who was so badly injured during fighting he couldn't stand, was strapped to a chair in the Execution Yard to face the firing squad. The ruthlessness of the killings outraged the public, both in Ireland and England, and boosted the nationalist cause.

The East Wing, modelled on London's Pentonville Prison, with metal catwalks suspended around a light-filled, vaulted room, allowed guards full view of all the cells. Graffiti, scratched and scrawled by prisoners in the cells, is moving stuff.

Guided tours to Kilmainham include an excellent museum; the prison chapel; the exercise and execution yards; and the dark, dank old wing. During the Great Famine, thousands of petty thieves, including children, were crammed in here.

See p103 for details.

>7 THE PLAY'S NOT THE ONLY THING

FOOD, BEER AND A DAMN GOOD PLAY: WHAT MORE DO YOU WANT?

Beckett, Synge, Shaw, Wilde…Dublin's not short of a theatrical genius or two, so a night at the theatre is absolutely necessary, daahling. But it'll take more than just the play, for any night out in Dublin has to involve food and booze somewhere along the way!

Start with the pretheatre special at Chapter One (p116), three-courses of gourmet delight at one of Dublin's best restaurants, in the basement of the Dublin Writers Museum (p111). What's really special about this place is that they'll pick your theatre tickets up for you and deliver them to your table. Then, it's off to either Ireland's national theatre, the world-famous Abbey (p118), or the Gate (p119; pictured above) – where James Mason and Orson Welles trod the boards in their youth – for the main event. When the curtain falls, make your way back to Chapter One for the remainder of your prandials, where you can dissect the merits of the show over dessert and coffee in the lounge, at the bar or at a table. To cap it off, make your way to one of the best traditional bars in town, the Sackville Lounge (p118), a favourite of thespians.

If you prefer to do your own ticketing, bookings can usually be made by credit card over the phone; you can collect your tickets just before the performance. Most plays begin at 8pm.

>8 GOING TO THE DOGS & OTHER SPORTING PURSUITS

LOSING YOUR MONEY AND YOUR VOICE IN SUPPORT OF SPORTING VICE

Dublin without sport is like…well, Guinness without the bishop's collar, so an afternoon or an evening in the company of Dubs pursuing their passion through bet and bellow is one of the best experiences you could ever have here.

Gaelic sports – hurling and football – are a national religion, and Dublin is home to the high cathedral of both games. The best time to go to Croke Park is during the summer and early autumn, when the stadium becomes a cauldron of passion, especially if Dublin is playing in the Senior Football Championship – they're not very good at hurling. But the best of the Senior Hurling Championship is on here too, with the likes of Kilkenny, Cork and Tipperary displaying their consummate skills to packed houses in excess of 70,000.

You may think that the dog track is the sole preserve of the gambling hound and other desperate types, but there's a surprise

in store, especially if you don't fancy the idea of standing against the rail while the drizzle dampens the printed hopes you hold in your hand and the greyhound in trap six isn't quite the speedster your money assumed him to be. No, you can experience the delight and dismay of a night at 'the dogs' from the comfort of the glass-enclosed stand, where dinner, fine wine and your very own waiter-cum-bookie will bring you refreshments and process your bets…at the table.

Croke Park is Dublin's most famous sporting venue, but there is a host of others.

Croke Park (Map p109, D1; ☎ 836 3222; www.crokepark.ie; Dublin 3; 🚌 3, 11, 11a, 16, 16a, 51a from O'Connell St; 🚊 Connolly Station)

Fairyhouse Racecourse (☎ 825 6167; www.fairyhouseracecourse.ie)

Harold's Cross Park (☎ 497 1081; 151 Harold's Cross Rd; 🚌 16, 16a, 19a, 49)

K Club (☎ 601 7200; www.kclub.ie; Straffan, Co Kildare)

Lansdowne Road Stadium (Map pp130-1, E2; ☎ 668 4601; Ballsbridge; 🚊 Lansdowne Rd)

Leopardstown (☎ 289 3607; www.leopardstown.com; Foxrock, Dublin 18; 🚌 from Eden Quay on race days)

Royal Dublin Society Showgrounds (Map pp130-1, E4; ☎ 668 0866; www.rds.ie; Ballsbridge; 🚌 5, 7, 7a, 8, 45; 🚊 Sandymount)

Shelbourne Greyhound Stadium (see p137; pictured above)

HIGHLIGHTS

>9 YOUR OWN PERSONAL RIVERDANCE

BUST AN IRISH MOVE ON THE DANCE FLOOR TO IMPRESS YOUR FRIENDS

Irish dancing looks impossibly fast and complicated, especially if your only experience of it is the phenomenon that is Riverdance. Two little facts: the Riverdance kids are good, but it ain't all that traditional; and learning the basics is not nearly as difficult as you think.

The Comhaltas Ceoltó iri Éireann (p136) – pronounced 'ko-ltass kee-oltory erin' and translated as the Organisation of Irish Musicians – is housed in the Cultúrlann na hÉireann (Irish Cultural Institute), the spiritual home of the traditional forms in Dublin, located in the southern suburb of Monkstown, which is easily reached from the city centre by DART. There are free, informal sessions of traditional music on Tuesday and Wednesday from 8pm; visitors are most welcome, where they can sit and tap their feet, get a bite to eat and have a few pints, all the while enjoying some of the best music around. But the real treat is on Friday night, where, for a nominal fee, you can participate in the *céilidh*, or group Irish dance, itself accompanied by live music. There are teachers on hand to help you with the basic steps, and if nothing else you can be guaranteed to learn how to stay on your feet during a jig, reel or square dance. It's an enormous amount of fun and one of the more memorable experiences of any trip to Dublin.

>DUBLIN DIARY

There is only a handful of weeks in Dublin where there isn't much to do, but even then you'll have plenty of options to make your own fun. No sooner does Christmas grind to a slow halt — sometime in January — then preparations begin for the mother of all piss-ups, ill-disguised as a celebration of Ireland's patron saint. Hardly a summer weekend goes by without there being some organised booty-shake or gourmet extravaganza — and the summer programme is eating ever more into autumn. In between the big events, there's a few quieter festivals to set your pulse racing.

Check out the live music around town

FEBRUARY

Dublin Film Festival
www.dubliniff.com

Local flicks, arty international films and advance screenings of mainstream movies make up the menu of the city's film festival.

Six Nations Championship
www.irishrugby.ie

The first rugby matches of the international calendar sees Ireland pitted against England, Scotland, Wales, France and Italy. Matches are played at Croke Park (Map p109, D1).

MARCH

St Patrick's Festival
www.stpatricksday.ie

The mother of all festivals. Hundreds of thousands gather to 'honour' St Patrick over four days around 17 March on city streets and in venues throughout the centre.

Howth Jazz Festival

Held on the Easter Bank Holiday in this pretty seaside suburb; most gigs are free.

APRIL

Handel's Messiah

A performance is held outside what was once Neal's Music Hall, Fishamble St, in Temple Bar, to mark the occasion of the sacred piece's first performance on April 13, 1742.

Convergence Festival
www.sustainable.ie

A 10-day green festival in Temple Bar focussed on renewable, sustainable living, with a diverse programme of workshops, talks and children's activities.

MAY

Mardi Gras
www.dublinpride.org

The last weekend of the month sees in Dublin's gay pride celebration, with a parade and other festivities.

Dublin Gay Theatre Festival
www.gaytheatre.ie

A fortnight devoted exclusively to gay theatre – plays by gay writers past and present that have a gay or gay-related theme.

JUNE

Dublin Writers Festival

www.dublinwritersfestival.com

Four-day literature festival attracting Irish and international writers.

Heineken Green Energy Festival

www.heineken.com

Four-day music festival that usually has an open-air concert in the grounds of Dublin Castle.

Women's Mini-Marathon

www.womensminimarathon.ie

A 10km charity run on the second Sunday of the month, attracting up to 35,000 participants – including some poorly disguised men.

JULY

Bloomsday (16th July)

www.jamesjoyce.ie

Celebrate *Ulysses* with readings (pictured below), wanderings, grub and costumes.

Diversions

www.templebar.ie

Street entertainment, kids' shows and workshops every Saturday in Meeting House Sq (see also p71).

Oxegen

www.oxegen.ie

Music festival over the July weekend closest to the 12th; manages to pack a few dozen heavyweight acts into its two-day line-up.

AUGUST

Dublin Horse Show
www.rds.ie

The horsey set trot down to the capital for the social highlight of the year, climaxing in the Aga Khan Cup, an international-class competition.

Dun Laoghaire Festival of World Cultures
www.festivalofworldcultures.com

Colourful multicultural music, art and theatre festival on the last weekend of the month.

SEPTEMBER

All-Ireland Finals
www.gaa.ie

Croke Park (Map p109, D1) goes wild with the hurling finals (second Sunday of the month) and Gaelic football finals (fourth Sunday).

Dublin Fringe Festival
www.fringefest.com

Lively fringe festival of theatre.

Bulmers International Comedy Festival
www.bulmerscomedy.ie

Best of Irish and international comics wringing out the laughs (pictured below).

OCTOBER

Dublin Theatre Festival

www.dublintheatrefestival.com

Europe's oldest theatre festival is a 2½-week showcase of Irish and international productions at various locations around town (pictured above).

Hallowe'en

Tens of thousands take to the city streets for a night-time parade, fireworks, street theatre, drinking and music to celebrate this traditional pagan festival in celebration of the dead, the end of the harvest and the Celtic New Year.

NOVEMBER

French Film Festival

www.irishfilm.ie

Organised by the French embassy and sponsored by Carte Noir, it showcases the best of French releases for the year.

Junior Dublin Film Festival

www.ifi.ie

A week-long showcase of the best efforts of the world's young filmmakers, the Irish Film Institute screens an exclusive selection of movies from all over.

DECEMBER

Christmas Dip @ the Forty Foot

Possibly the most hardcore hangover cure known to man, this event takes place at 11am on Christmas Day at the famous swimming spot below Martello Tower (pictured below) in Sandycove that is home to the James Joyce Museum (p133).

Leopardstown Races

www.leopardstown.com

Historic and hugely popular racing festival at one of Europe's loveliest courses, from 26 to 30 December.

WHEN IN DUBLIN...

Even if you're not in town for one of the fixed major events, keep your eyes and ears peeled for other flexible dates on the fun calendar. The **Temple Bar Trad Festival of Irish Music & Culture** (www .templebartrad.com) is a mouthful, but it's three days of quality music at the beginning of the year. **Tastefest** (www .rds.ie) is an actual mouthful of gourmet delicacies that takes over the Royal Dublin Society around March. In summer, look out for the **Street Performance World Championship** where the best pavement entertainers go head-to-head; in 2006 more than 26,000 people attended the inaugural festival.

>ITINERARIES

Guinness Storehouse (p102)

ITINERARIES

DAY ONE

Start early at Trinity College (p40) then ramble over to George's St Arcade (p85) to nose about the record and book stalls. For lunch, bag an outside table at La Maison des Gourmets (p91), then ramble up the Guinness Storehouse (p102) for an hour or so. While you're in that neck of the woods, mosey around the Liberties (Map pp100-1, G3) not missing Mother's Tankship (p105) before heading back to town for dinner on the terrace at Eden (p73) and a few scoops at the Stag's Head (p95).

DAY TWO

Start at the Chester Beatty Library (p82) in Dublin Castle (p82), pitstopping at Chez Max (p89) for a coffee and *pain au chocolat* (chocolate croissant). Browse the shops around Grafton St (Map p39, B3) before a visit to the National Museum (p59) or National Gallery (p57). Catch evensong at Christ Church Cathedral (p99) before dinner at Gruel (p74) and a comedy show at the International Bar (p49).

DAY THREE

Pick up some ethnic food on a stroll around Moore St (Map p109, B4) and Parnell St (Map p109, B4) before dropping into James Joyce Centre (p112) for a walking tour or across to Cobalt Café & Gallery (p116) for some warm soda bread and tea. Then head west to the Irish Museum of Modern Art (IMMA; p102) and Kilmainham Gaol (p103) for a cultural fix. Enjoy an early dinner at Fallon & Byrne (p90) before a show at the Project Arts Centre (p79) in Temple Bar.

RAINY DAY

Uncertain, inclement weather has made Dublin a city of interiors. You could spend hours perusing the collections at the National Museum (p59) and National Gallery (p57), but don't miss out on the magnificent Chester Beatty Library (p82). A wet-day pick-me-up across the street at the Queen of Tarts (p75) is a must, before heading into Temple Bar and a

---

Top George's St Arcade (p85) **Bottom** National Gallery of Ireland (p57)

ITINERARIES

visit to the Gallery of Photography (p68). By now, all cultured up, it's time to enjoy the rain like all Dubliners do, with a pint at the pub – the Stag's Head (p95) should do the trick.

OFF THE BEATEN TRACK

Dublin's city centre can get horribly congested with both people and cars, but it's not difficult to find some peace. For a real escape head to the seaside suburbs, or try some more central idylls:

> Farmleigh's pleasure gardens (p124)
> South Wall walk to the lighthouse (pictured above)
> Prospect Cemetery (p140)
> The outdoor café at the Dublin Writers Museum (p111)
> Iveagh Gardens (p53)
> Blessington St City Basin (Map pp122-3, G2)

FORWARD PLANNING

During summer, queues can be horrendous at popular attractions; arrive early. Most fee-paying sights offer discounts to students, the elderly, children and families. If you're serious about sightseeing, buy the Dublin Pass (see p170) as soon as you set foot in the airport – it'll give a you free ride on the Aircoach.

Two weeks before you go Advance purchase is a must if you want to take in a hit play at the Abbey Theatre (p118) or the Gate Theatre (p119) – a couple of weeks' ahead should be plenty of time. Ditto if you want to watch a game at Croke Park (p21), especially for the latter stages of the championship.

Three days before you go The very best and newest of Dublin's restaurants can be pretty tough to get a table at if you leave it to the last minute, but you shouldn't have any problems if you book a couple of days in advance.

PINTS A PLENTY

How many you have is entirely up to you, but we suggest you kick off your journey into the unknown at the Globe (p94) before going for an artsy pint in atmospheric Grogan's Castle Lounge (p94). From there, stop off at the Long Hall (p95) before walking south into the heart of SoDa. Wexford and Camden Sts have the wonderful Carnival (p94) and Anseo (p92). Back in the city centre, you should at least pop your head into Ron Black's (p50) before heading back towards SoDa, having a drink in the Stag's Head (p95) and then – oiled up to the gills – venturing into the mayhem of Temple Bar. The Palace Bar (p77) is terrific, and who knows, there might even be a traditional music session on upstairs.

DUBLIN FOR FREE

You can keep your money in your pocket at all of the national museums and galleries, including superb IMMA (p102), but also worth keeping in mind is a visit to the Government Buildings (p53) – pick up your visitor ticket from the National Gallery. You'll have to book in advance, but the tour of Leinster House (p57) – where the parliament sits – is also free, as are, of course, all of the city's Georgian squares. Be sure to take a peek at the Bank of Ireland (p40) on College Green – once home to the first Irish Parliament – before wandering about the evocative campus of Trinity College (p40), perhaps stopping into the Douglas Hyde Gallery (p40).

>NEIGHBOURHOODS

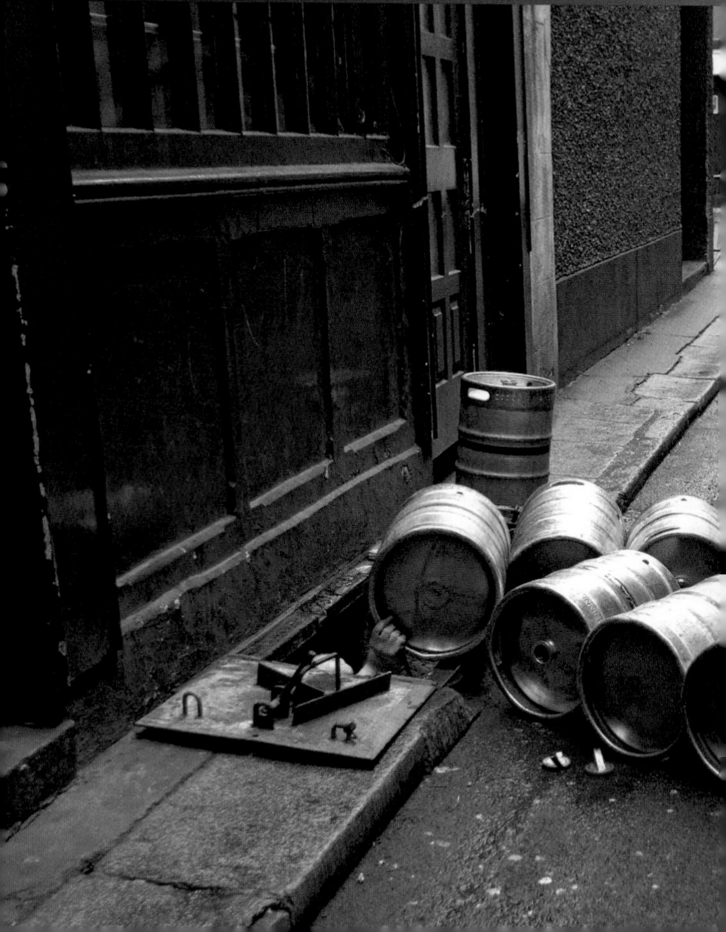

Empty Guinness barrels, alleyway south of Dame St

NEIGHBOURHOODS

Dublin is a dream to get around: a chock-a-block capital city with the intimacy of a big town. Much of this is down to its compact size – the city centre is quite small, with a clear focus. You'll find that shoe-power is the best way of getting around most of the time. Conveniently, the majority of sights are clustered around the city centre, while the ones that demand a little legwork are genuinely worth the effort – and are easy to get to in any case. Unless you're driving – and for God's sake what are you doing that for? – you should flow through the city like a breeze, barely putting a dent in your soles.

To make it even easier to navigate, we've divided the city into nine bite-sized chunks – six of them south of the Liffey where most of tourist life is lived. 'Around Grafton Street' covers the area surrounding Dublin's main recreational thoroughfare, 'Temple Bar' is its designated tourist heart and 'SoDa' its cutting edge. 'Georgian Dublin' is a large sprawling area surrounding Merrion Sq and St Stephen's Green, containing many of Ireland's national museums. 'Kilmainham & the Liberties', to the west of the city centre, are laden with sights and character but light on social opportunities.

North of the Liffey, 'Around O'Connell Street' takes in the sights and attractions of the city's one-time centre and still its grandest avenue – after years in the doldrums it's redecorating its way back into the spotlight. To the west, 'Smithfield & Phoenix Park' takes in the more traditional neighbourhoods and the city's giant-sized park, while 'Beyond the Royal Canal' is workaday Dublin, which has a host of very impressive sights. 'Beyond the Grand Canal' contains the wealthy inner southern suburbs, with some of Dublin's trendiest eateries. Lying north and south of the Royal and Grand Canals, respectively (see the 'Worth the Trip' boxed texts in those sections), are some pretty seaside villages that make for delightful mini-excursions out of the city.

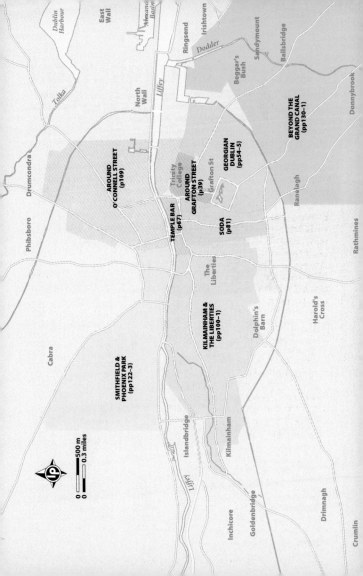

AROUND O'CONNELL STREET (p109)

TEMPLE BAR (p67)

Trinity College

AROUND GRAFTON STREET (p39)

Grafton St

GEORGIAN DUBLIN (pp54–5)

SODA (p81)

BEYOND THE GRAND CANAL (pp130–1)

KILMAINHAM & THE LIBERTIES (pp100–1)

The Liberties

SMITHFIELD & PHOENIX PARK (pp122–3)

Dublin Harbour

East Wall

Ringsend

Irishtown

Dodder

Sandymount

Ballsbridge

North Wall

Liffey

Beggar's Bush

Donnybrook

Drumcondra

Tolka

Ranelagh

Phibsboro

Rathmines

Cabra

Harold's Cross

Dolphin's Barn

Islandbridge

Kilmainham

Inchicore

Goldenbridge

Drimnagh

Crumlin

Liffey

0   500 m
0   0.3 miles

>AROUND GRAFTON STREET

Dublin's affluent heart is this short, pedestrianised street that snakes its way through the retail heartland from Trinity College to St Stephen's Green. No motors allowed, but there isn't room for them anyway, for Grafton St literally throbs with streetlife – so much so that you'll have to get up pretty early not to get lost in the throng that comes to shop, stare and stroll.

Named after the 17th-century Duke of Grafton, who owned much of these parts, Grafton St proper starts from the area known as College Green, directly in front of the elegant façades of Trinity College (one of world's most prestigious universities), and the Bank of Ireland (built to house Ireland's first parliament). An unremarkable statue of Molly Malone leads us, bosoms first, to the pedestrianised street, which is Grafton St.

AROUND GRAFTON STREET

◉ SEE
Bank of Ireland.............1 B2
Douglas Hyde Gallery.....2 B3
Solomon Gallery.............3 A3
Trinity College.............4 C3

⌂ SHOP
Alias Tom.................5 B4
Angles...............(see 26)
Appleby.................6 B4
Avoca Handweavers.......7 B3
Brown Thomas...........8 B3
BT2.....................9 B4
Cathach Books.........10 B4
Chica................(see 26)
Decent Cigar
Emporium.............11 B4
Design Centre......(see 20)
Dunnes Stores.........12 A4
Great Outdoors........13 A4
H Danker..............14 B4

Hodges Figgis........15 B3
Kilkenny.............16 B3
Magills..............17 A4
Murder Ink...........18 B4
Optica...............19 B4
Powerscourt Centre....20 A3
Rhinestones..........21 A3
St Stephen's Green
Shopping Centre......22 A5
Sheridans
Cheesemongers.......23 B4
Waterstone's.........24 B3
Weir & Sons..........25 B3
Westbury Mall........26 A4

🍴 EAT
Avoca Café..........(see 7)
Aya................(see 8)
Bleu.................27 B5
Eddie Rocket's......(see 37)
Gotham Café.........28 B4

Harry's Café.........29 B5
La Cave..............30 B4
La Stampa............31 B4
Mackerel...........(see 40)
Nude.................32 B3
Steps of Rome........33 A4
Thornton's...........34 A5
Trocadero............35 A3
Venu.................36 B4

🍸 DRINK
Kehoe's..............37 B4
O'Neill's............38 A3
Ron Black's..........39 B4

★ PLAY
Bewley's Café Theatre..40 B4
Gaiety Theatre.......41 A4
International Bar.....42 A3
Lillies Bordello.....43 B3
Screen...............44 C2

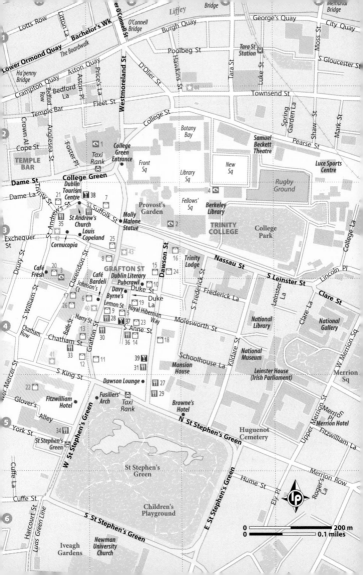

SEE

BANK OF IRELAND

☎ 671 1488, 677 6801; www.bankof
ireland.ie; College Green; admission free;
🕙 10am-4pm Mon-Wed & Fri, to 5pm Thu;
🚌 all city-centre buses; 🚆 Tara Street;
♿ limited

Built for the Irish Parliament, the
Bank of Ireland moved in after the
Act of Union in 1801. Though the
House of Commons was remodelled, the House of Lords survived
intact. Its Irish oak woodwork,
mahogany standing clock and
tapestries are worth a look. Free
tours are held on Tuesday at
10.30am, 11.30am and 1.45pm.

Trinity College

DOUGLAS HYDE GALLERY

☎ 896 1116; www.douglashydegallery
.com; Trinity College; admission free;
🕙 11am-6pm Mon-Wed & Fri, to 7pm
Thu, to 4.45pm Sat; 🚌 all city-centre
buses; 🚆 Pearse Station, Tara Street

This is one of those galleries that
seems to have escaped the public
radar, partly because of its location on-campus at Trinity. Its ambitious contemporary programme
sticks firmly in the cutting-edge
camp and exhibitions here are
often 'enhanced' with film, live
music or performance-driven side
shows.

SOLOMON GALLERY

☎ 679 4237; www.solomongallery.com;
Powerscourt Centre, S William St; admission free; 🕙 10am-5.30pm Mon-Sat;
🚌 all city-centre buses

In a restored Georgian salon on
the top floor of the Powerscourt
Centre (p45), Solomon Gallery,
popular with Dublin's glitterati,
has a reputation for showing fine
figurative art including painting, ceramics, glass and mixed
media. Along with contemporary
pieces are traditional Irish period
paintings.

TRINITY COLLEGE

☎ 677 2941, 30 min walking tours
608 1724; College Green grounds; admission grounds free, Book of Kells €8/7,
under 12 free, walking tours incl entry
to Book of Kells €10.50; 🕙 grounds

8am-midnight, Old Library/Book of Kells 9.30am-5pm Mon-Sat, to 4.30pm Sun, from noon Sun Oct-May; ⏲ **walking tours** dept Front Sq from 10.15am every 40min Apr-Oct; 🚉 Pearse Station, Tara Street; ♿ **good**

The country's most famous university is an oasis of Victorian tranquility and gentility in the middle of the city. Founded by Elizabeth I in 1592, most of the stunning buildings and land-scaped squares date from the 18th and 19th centuries, but the campus' single biggest attraction is much, much older – queue up to gape at the *Book of Kells*, one of the world's most extraordinary illuminated manuscripts. See also p10.

SHOP

◻ ALIAS TOM

☎ 671 544; 3 Duke Lane; ⏲ 9.30am-6pm Mon-Wed, Fri & Sat, to 8pm Thu; 🚌 all cross-city; 🚉 St Stephen's Green

This is Dublin's best designer menswear store, where friendly staff guide you through casuals by bling labels Burberry and YSL Rive Gauche. Downstairs you'll find classic tailored suits and Patrick Cox shoes.

◻ ANGLES

☎ 679 1964; Westbury Mall; ⏲ 10am-6pm Mon-Wed, Fri & Sat, to 7pm Thu; 🚌 all cross-city; 🚉 St Stephen's Green

ARMCHAIR SHOPPING
Want to avoid the leg-numbing march of the pavements in search of a bargain or much sought-after souvenir? Relax, grab a cuppa and do it online.
www.buy4now.ie A catch-all website of Irish shops that offers nearly everything you can think of, from ski holidays to boxed sets of *Fair City*.
www.shopirishwithmoytura.com Irish-themed items include *bodráns* (Irish drums), Paddy's day souvenirs and Irish biscuits.

You won't find Claddagh rings or charm bracelets here, just cabinets full of handmade, contemporary Irish jewellery, most of it by up-and-coming Dublin craftspeople. Commissions are taken and items can be sent on to you abroad.

◻ APPLEBY

☎ 679 9572; 5-6 Johnson's Ct; ⏲ 9.30am-5.30pm Mon-Wed & Fri, to 7pm Thu, to 6pm Sat; 🚌 all cross-city; 🚉 St Stephen's Green

Renowned for the high quality of its gold and silver jewellery, which tends towards more conventional designs, this is the place to shop for serious stuff – diamond rings, sapphire-encrusted cufflinks and Raymond Weil watches.

☐ AVOCA HANDWEAVERS

☎ 677 4215; 11-13 Suffolk St; ⏱ 10am-6pm Mon-Wed, Fri & Sat, to 8pm Thu, 11am-6pm Sun; 🚌 all cross-city

Combining clothing, homewares, a basement food hall and an excellent top-floor café, Avoca promotes a stylish but homy brand of modern Irish life. Many of the garments sold here are woven, knitted and naturally dyed at its Wicklow factory. The children's section, which features unusual knits, fairy outfits, bee-covered gumboots and dinky toys, is fantastic.

☐ BROWN THOMAS

☎ 605 6666; 95 Grafton St; ⏱ 9am-8pm Mon-Wed & Fri, to 9pm Thu, to 7pm Sat, 10am-7pm Sun; 🚌 all cross-city; 🚇 St Stephen's Green

Soak up the Jo Malone–laden rarefied atmosphere of Dublin's most exclusive store where presentation is virtually artistic. Here you'll find a selection of fantastic cosmetics, shoes to die for, exotic homewares and a host of Irish and international fashion labels such as Balenciaga, Stella McCarthy, Lainey Keogh and Philip Treacy. The café on the 2nd-floor is small and surprisingly relaxed, as is Brown's Bar in the basement.

☐ BT2

☎ 679 5666; 88 Grafton St; ⏱ 9am-6.30pm Mon-Wed & Fri, to 9pm Thu, to 7pm Sat, 10am-6.30pm Sun; 🚌 all cross-city; 🚇 St Stephen's Green

Brown Thomas' young and funky offshoot, with high-end casuals for men and women and a juice bar upstairs overlooking Grafton St. Brands include DKNY, Custom, Diesel, Ted Baker and Tommy Hilfiger.

☐ CATHACH BOOKS

☎ 671 8676; 10 Duke St; ⏱ 9.30am-5.45pm Mon-Sat; 🚌 all cross-city

Dusty rare editions of Irish literature and history, including works by Wilde, Joyce, Yeats and Beckett, and a large selection of signed first editions await you in one of Dublin's best antiquarian bookshops.

☐ CHICA

☎ 671 9836; Westbury Mall; ⏱ 10am-5.30pm Tue, Wed, Fri & Sat, to 7pm Thu; 🚌 all cross-city; 🚇 St Stephen's Green

A one-stop shop for all your chic party needs. This little boutique will sort out your wardrobe with slinky, wow-factor dresses from Sika, Hunter Gatherers or New York label Candela.

☐ DECENT CIGAR EMPORIUM

☎ 671 6451; 46 Grafton St; ⏱ 10am-6pm Mon-Wed, Fri & Sat, to 8pm Thu, 1.30-5.30pm Sun; 🚌 all city-centre; 🚇 St Stephen's Green

When the clamour of Grafton St gets too much, slip up this discreet staircase, recline in a plush leather armchair and run your nose along a sweet hand-rolled, long-filler cigar over a glass of decent red wine or a cup of Illy coffee.

📷 DESIGN CENTRE
☎ 679 5718; Powerscourt Centre; 🕐 10am-6pm Mon-Wed & Fri, to 8pm Thu, 9.30am-6pm Sat, noon-6pm Sun; 🚌 all cross-city; 🚊 St Stephen's Green
Mostly dedicated to Irish designer women's wear, with well-made, classic suits, evening wear and knitwear. Irish labels include Louise Kennedy, Pauric Sweeney, Mairead Whisker and Philip Treacy. Martine Sitbon, Kenzo and Matthew Williamson also get a look in.

📷 DUNNES STORES
☎ 671 4629; 62 Grafton St; 🕐 9am-6.30pm Mon-Wed, Fri & Sat, to 9pm Thu, noon-6pm Sun; 🚌 all cross-city; 🚊 St Stephen's Green
A favourite choice with Irish mothers for its affordable everyday family clothing. The Savida fashion range is remarkably on the pulse, though, and has an excellent homewares department. Look for branches across the city including the new **Dunne Home** (Map p81, C2; ☎ 415 5044; S Great Georges St).

📷 GREAT OUTDOORS
☎ 679 4293; 20 Chatham St; 🕐 9.30am-5.30pm Mon-Wed, Fri & Sat, to 8pm Thu; 🚌 all cross-city; 🚊 St Stephen's Green
Dublin's best outdoors store, with gear for hiking, camping, surfing,

Grafton St

mountaineering, swimming and more. Also has an info-laden noticeboard.

🏠 H DANKER
☎ 677 4009; 10 S Anne St; ☽ 9.30am-5pm Mon-Sat; 🚌 all cross-city
Chock-full of exquisite treasures, this shop specialises in Irish and English antique silver, jewellery and *objets d'art*.

🏠 HODGES FIGGIS
☎ 677 4754; 57 Dawson St; ☽ 9am-7pm Mon-Wed & Fri, to 8pm Thu, to 6pm Sat, noon-6pm Sun; 🚌 all cross-city
The most complete bookshop in town has books on every conceivable subject for every kind of reader. A very wide range of Irish-interest titles are found on the ground floor.

🏠 KILKENNY
☎ 677 7066; 5-6 Nassau St; ☽ 8.30am-6pm Mon-Wed, & Fri, to 8pm Thu, to 6pm Sat; 11am-6pm Sun 🚌 all cross-city
A large, long-running repository for contemporary, innovative Irish crafts, including multicoloured, modern Irish knits, designer clothing, Orla Kiely bags and some lovely silver jewellery. The beautiful glassware and pottery is sourced from workshops around the country. A great place for presents.

🏠 MAGILLS
☎ 671 3830; 14 Clarendon St; ☽ 9.30am-5.45pm Mon-Sat; 🚌 all cross-city; 🚊 St Stephen's Green
With its characterful old façade and tiny dark interior, Magills' old-world charm reminds you how Clarendon St must have once looked. Family-run, you get the distinct feeling that every Irish and French cheese, olive oil, packet of Italian pasta and salami was hand-picked.

🏠 MURDER INK
☎ 677 7570; 15 Dawson St; ☽ 10am-5.30pm Mon-Sat, noon-5pm Sun; 🚌 all cross-city; 🚊 St Stephen's Green
All manner of murder mystery and crime novels are in this specialist bookshop that has categorisation down to a fine art – choose from historical mystery, romantic crime, sci-fi mystery, true crime and more.

CONSUMER R&R
There's no need to shop till you drop while pounding the streets of Dublin. Several stores have quiet and comfortable cafés where you can refuel, take stock and plan your next move.
> Avoca Handweavers (p42)
> Brown Thomas (p42)
> Kilkenny (left)
> Powerscourt Centre (right)
> Winding Stair (p115)

☐ OPTICA
☎ 677 4705; 1 Royal Hibernian Way; ☽ 9.30am-5.30pm Mon-Wed, Fri & Sat, to 6.30pm Thu; 🚌 all cross-city; 🚋 St Stephen's Green

Who says guys don't make passes at girls who wear glasses? Knock 'em dead in head-turning specs and shades by Chanel, D&G, Stella McCartney and Oliver Peoples.

☐ POWERSCOURT CENTRE
☎ 679 4144; 59 S William St; ☽ 10am-6pm Mon-Wed & Fri, to 8pm Thu, 9am-6pm Sat, noon-6pm Sun; 🚌 all cross-city; 🚋 St Stephen's Green

This upmarket shopping mall in an 18th-century town house is where discerning shoppers quietly visit boutiques, beauty salons and the 1st-floor art, craft and antique shops. The Design Centre and FCUK are also here, as are Solomon Gallery, a great vegetarian restaurant and a wig store. **Mimo** (☎ 679 7789), the courtyard restaurant, is a pleasant spot to gather yourself.

☐ RHINESTONES
☎ 679 0759; 18 St Andrew's St; ☽ 9am-6.30pm Mon-Wed, Fri & Sat, to 8pm Thu, noon-6pm Sun; 🚌 all cross-city

Exceptionally fine antique and quirky costume jewellery from the 1920s to 1970s, with pieces priced from €25 to €2000. Victorian jet, 1950s enamel, Art Deco turquoise, 1930s mother-of-pearl, cut-glass and rhinestone necklaces, bracelets, brooches and rings are displayed by colour in old-fashioned cabinets.

☐ ST STEPHEN'S GREEN SHOPPING CENTRE
☎ 478 0888; cnr S King St & W St Stephen's Green; ☽ 9am-6pm Mon-Wed, Fri & Sat, to 9pm Thu, noon-6pm Sun; 🚌 all cross-city; 🚋 St Stephen's Green

A 1980s version of a 19th-century shopping arcade, the dramatic, balconied interior and central courtyard are a bit too grand for the nondescript chain stores within. Here you'll find a Boots, Benetton and large Dunnes Store with supermarket as well as last season designer warehouse TK Maxx.

☐ SHERIDANS CHEESEMONGERS
☎ 679 3143; 11 S Anne St; ☽ 10am-6pm Mon-Fri, from 9.30am Sat; 🚌 all cross-city; 🚋 St Stephen's Green

If heaven were a cheese shop, this would be it. Wooden shelves are laden with rounds of farmhouse cheeses, sourced by Kevin and Seamus Sheridan, who have almost single-handedly revived the practice of cheese-making in Ireland. You can taste any one of the 60 cheeses on display and, while you're at it, you can also pick up some wild Irish salmon, Italian pastas and olives.

☐ WATERSTONE'S

☎ 679 1415; 7 Dawson St; ☺ 9am-7pm Mon-Wed & Fri, to 8pm Thu, to 6.30pm Sat, noon-6pm Sun; 🚌 all cross-city
Although it is large and multi-storied, Waterstone's somehow manages to maintain that snugly, hide-in-a-corner ambience that book lovers adore. The broad selection of books is supplemented by five bookcases of Irish fiction, in addition to poetry, drama, politics and history. Waterstone's hosts book-signings every Thursday evening; check the board outside for details.

☐ WEIR & SONS

☎ 677 9678; 96-99 Grafton St; ☺ 9am-5.30pm Mon-Wed, Fri & Sat, to 8pm Thu; 🚌 all cross-city
The largest jeweller in Ireland, this huge store on Grafton St first opened in 1869 and still has its original wooden cabinets and a workshop on the premises. There's new and antique Irish jewellery (including Celtic designs) and a huge selection of watches, Irish crystal, porcelain, leather and travel goods.

☐ WESTBURY MALL

Clarendon St; ☺ 10am-6pm Mon-Sat, noon-5pm Sun; 🚌 all cross-city; 🚊 St Stephen's Green
Wedged between the five-star Westbury Hotel and the expensive jewellery stores of Johnson's Ct, this small mall has a handful of pricey, specialist shops selling everything from Persian rugs to buttons and lace or tasteful children's wooden toys.

🍴 EAT

🍴 AVOCA CAFÉ *Café*   €€

☎ 672 6019; Avoca Handweavers, 11-13 Suffolk St; ☺ 10am-5pm Mon-Sat, from 10.30am Sun; 🚌 all cross-city; ♿ 👶 Ⓥ
This airy café was one of Dublin's best-kept secrets – hidden above Avoca Handweavers (p42) – until discovered by the Ladies Who Lunch. Battle your way to a table past the designer shopping bags, where you'll relish the delicious, rustic delights of organic shepherd's pie, roast lamb with couscous, or sumptuous salads. There's a secret takeaway salad bar and hot counter in the basement.

🍴 AYA *Japanese*   €€€

☎ 677 1544; 49-52 Clarendon St; ☺ 10.30am-11pm Mon-Sat, noon-10pm Sun; 🚌 all cross-city; 👶 Ⓥ
Attached to the swanky shop Brown Thomas (p42), this Japanese restaurant is the city centre's best. There's a revolving sushi bar where you can eat your fill for €25 between 5pm and 9pm (maximum 55 minutes, excluding Thursday and Saturday) or go à la

carte from the great menu. Pick up takeaway or specialist products at the Japanese minimart next door.

¥¶ BLEU *Bistro* €€€
☎ 676 7015; Joshua House, Dawson St; ☙ noon-3pm & 6-11pm; ☒ St Stephen's Green; ♿ ♨ Ⓥ

With black leather seats and massive windows overlooking swanky Dawson St you can see and be seen at Eamon O'Reilly's upmarket outpost of modern Irish cuisine. Confit of pork belly, swordfish with coconut and caraway and – that trademark of trendy menus – fish and chips keep upmarket preclubber's hunger pangs at bay for a few hours.

LATE-NIGHT EATS
Most kitchens shut around 10pm, but there are some places where you can feed the beast a little later. **Eddie Rocket's** (☎ 679 7340; 7 S Anne St; ☙ 7.30am-1am, to 4.30am Sun-Thu) is a saviour for many a hungry Dub. This cheap and cheerful 1950s-style US diner dishes out anything from breakfast to burgers and fries. Other late-night options are more upmarket, such as Trocadero (p49), which jumps till late, and La Stampa (p48), where hip young things munch on steak and chips to stave off that inevitable hangover.

¥¶ GOTHAM CAFÉ *Café* €€
☎ 679 5266; 8 S Anne St; ☙ noon-midnight Mon-Sat, noon-10.30pm Sun; ☒ St Stephen's Green; ♨ Ⓥ

A vibrant, youthful place decorated with framed Rolling Stones album covers, Gotham extends its New York theme to its delicious pizzas named after districts in the Big Apple. Chinatown and Noho are among our favourites, or you can opt for pasta, crostini or Asian salads. And, hey, they love kids here.

¥¶ HARRY'S CAFÉ *Café* €€
☎ 639 4889; 22 Dawson St; ☙ noon-4pm Mon, to 11pm Tue-Sat, to 10.30pm Sun; ☒ all cross-city; ☒ St Stephen's Green; ♨ Ⓥ

Harry's has a great wine list, many of which you'll see mounted on the bare brick walls of this friendly place. House specialities include organic beef burgers or bangers and mash, but the baked Mediterranean stack oozing melted goat's cheese is our favourite.

¥¶ LA CAVE *French wine bar* €€
☎ 679 4409; 28 S Anne St; ☙ 12.30pm-late Mon-Sat, 6pm-late Sun; ☒ all cross-city; ☒ St Stephen's Green; ♨ to 6pm

From the outside, La Cave looks like it might be an adult

bookshop or a gangster pool hall. Wind your way downstairs and you'll discover a chic, Paris-style wine bar with crimson walls, tiny tables and a packed crowd shouting over the Brazilian salsa music. The food is OK, but you're really here for the setting and the superb wine list.

🍴 LA STAMPA
Modern European €€€
☎ 677 8611; 35 Dawson St; ⏲ 6pm-midnight Sun-Thu, to 12.30am Fri & Sat; 🚆 St Stephen's Green; 🚶 🚻 V

Set in the opulent 19th-century La Stampa Hotel, the décor here is quite gorgeous – richly coloured drapery and bright, modern artworks. The food ranges from seared scallop chips to beef Rossini on spinach.

🍴 MACKEREL *Seafood* €€€
☎ 672 7719; www.mackerel.ie; Bewley's Café Theatre; ⏲ noon-4pm & 5-10pm; 🚆 Stephen's Green; 🚶 fair; 🚻

In the two years since it opened, Mackerel has won some serious awards, not least for the consistently high-standard menu that sees Eleanor Walsh of Eden fame (see p73) take fish from boat to plate with minimum fuss and maximum taste. Roast red snapper with chorizo and fava bean is sublime.

🍴 NUDE *Café* €
☎ 677 4804; 21 Suffolk St; ⏲ 8am-9pm Mon-Wed, Fri & Sat, to 9.30pm Thu, to 7pm Sun; 🚆 all cross-city; 🚶 V

With juice bars a-go-go in the city, modernist Nude may no longer be the rarity it once was, but it still maintains its own unique identity. Owned by Bono's brother, it takes the fast-food experience to a delicious and healthy extreme offering hot Asian wraps, bean casseroles and spirulina-spiked juices to go or have on the (plastic-free) spot.

🍴 STEPS OF ROME *Italian* €
☎ 670 5630; Chatham St; ⏲ 10am-midnight; 🚆 all cross-city; 🚆 St Stephen's Green; 🚻 V

Take away rustic pizza slices or sit in and rub elbows with the Italian frat pack over a hot bowl of linguine in this tiny kerbside café. It's always packed and you can't book, but service is smart so you'll usually get a table after a few minutes' wait.

🍴 THORNTON'S
Modern European €€€€
☎ 478 7008; Fitzwilliam Hotel, 128 W St Stephen's Green; ⏲ 12.30-2pm & 7-10pm Tue-Sat; 🚆 all cross-city; 🚆 St Stephen's Green; 🚶 🚻

So they dropped a Michelin star (down to one) in 2006, but who's

BOY IN THE HOOD

New Yorker Des Bishop moved to Ireland at 14. By his 20s he had learned to turn his outsider status to good effect in a stand-up routine that cashed in on his wry, outspoken observations about Irish life. Two biting socially-aware TV series followed that catapulted him to Irish stardom. One, *Joy in the Hood*, followed his passionate spell teaching marginalised people around the country to be comics. True to his roots he is still Comedy Club MC at Dublin's International Bar (below).

counting? Kevin Thornton is still considered the finest chef to come out of Ireland in decades. Set menus here offer reasonably good value considering what you're getting: a chance to experience the sublime creations of his team, along with impeccable service, and a seat overlooking St Stephen's Green.

🍴 TROCADERO
Traditional Irish   €€€
☎ 677 5545; 3 St Andrew's St; 🕑 5pm-midnight Mon-Sat; 🚇 all cross-city; ♿
Seedy burlesque venue from the street, flamboyant *belle époque* bar inside, the Troc is a favourite of thespians, media types and the odd drag queen. Robert Doggett is one of the most charming maîtres d in town. Dinners are

supremely unfashionable but that somehow adds to the charm. The pretheatre menu is popular, but stick around late to see the real action.

🍴 VENU *Modern European*   €€€
☎ 670 6755; S Anne St; 🕑 noon-11pm; 🚇 all cross-city; 🚇 St Stephen's Green; ♿ ♿ Ⓥ
This place could have been all fur coat and no knickers. Charles Guilbaud, son of food legend Patrick, opened his own bolthole in summer '06 to bated breath. There was a collective sigh of relief however as foodies flocked to the nightclubesque brasserie to tuck appreciatively into dishes such as grilled salmon with lime, and fillet of beef. Excellent value for top fodder.

🍸 DRINK
🍸 INTERNATIONAL BAR
☎ 677 9250; 23 Wicklow St; admission €10/8; 🕑 comedy Mon, Wed-Sat 9pm; 🚇 all cross-city
A fantastic pub with stained glass and mirrors, famous for long-running comedy nights and jazz and blues on Tuesday. Ardal O'Hanlon, who played Dougal in *Father Ted*, began his career here doing stand-up comedy, as did TV comics Dara O'Briain and Des Bishop.

▼ KEHOE'S

☎ 677 8312; 9 S Anne St; 🚌 all cross-city; 🚶 to 7pm

One of Dublin's most atmospheric pubs, featuring a beautiful Victorian bar, Kehoe's has comfy snugs and plenty of other little nooks and crannies in which to secrete yourself. Upstairs, drinks are served in what was once the publican's living room – and it looks it.

▼ O'NEILL'S

☎ 679 3671; 2 Suffolk St; 🚌 all cross-city; 🚶 to 6pm

A labyrinthine old pub situated near Trinity College, O'Neill's dates from the late 19th century, though a tavern has stood on this site for more than 300 years. The odd combination of students and stockbrokers lends the place a chaotic air and it offers good food too.

▼ RON BLACK'S

☎ 672 8231; 37 Dawson St; 🕑 11am-11.30pm Mon-Wed, to 2am Thu-Sat, noon-11pm Sun; 🚌 10, 14, 14a, 15; 🚶 to 7pm

Despite its cavernous size, this upmarket watering hole manages to retain an inviting atmosphere, thanks to plenty of warm wooden panelling, leather sofas and huge soft lights. The newly opened champagne bar upstairs attracts suity young men and smart-dressed girls who aren't afraid to flash their cash.

⭐ PLAY

☆ BEWLEY'S CAFÉ THEATRE

☎ 086 878 4001; 78-79 Grafton St; admission €8-15; 🕑 12.50pm & 8.30pm; 🚇 Stephen's Green; ♿ good; 🚶

The theatre space in the beautiful Oriental Room at Bewley's Café is long established for its excellent lunchtime drama (admission includes soup and sandwich) as well as an evening programme featuring rigorous drama, comedy and jazz.

☆ GAIETY THEATRE

☎ 677 1717; www.gaietytheatre.net; S King St; 🕑 box office 10am-7pm Mon-Sat; 🚌 all cross-city; 🚇 St Stephen's Green; 🚶

Opened in 1871, this Victorian theatre was restored to its former glory several years ago. Its repertoire is diverse, from modern plays, musicals, comedies and panto to Shakespeare. Opera Ireland has a season here. On Friday and Saturday nights the venue is taken over by salsa and soul clubs until 4am.

☆ LILLIES BORDELLO

☎ 679 9204; www.lilliesbordello.ie; Adam Ct; admission €10-20; 🕑 11pm-3am; 🚌 all cross-city

Grafton St

Lillies is strictly for Big Hairs, wannabes and visiting rock stars. Don't think you'll get to rub shoulders celebs though, as they'll be whisked out of view and into the VIP room in a flash. As you might expect, the music is mostly safe and commercial.

☆ SCREEN

☎ 672 5500; 2 Townsend St; admission before/after 6pm €6.50/8.50; ⏰ 2-10.30pm; 🚌 5, 7, 7a, 8, 14; 🚉 Tara Street; ♿

Between Trinity College and O'Connell Bridge, Screen shows fairly good art-house and indie films on its three screens.

>GEORGIAN DUBLIN

East of Grafton St is where much of moneyed Dublin works and plays, amid the magnificent Georgian splendour thrown up during Dublin's 18th-century prime. When James Fitzgerald, the earl of Kildare, built his mansion south of the Liffey, he was mocked for his foolhardy move into the wilds. But Jimmy Fitz had a nose for real estate: 'Where I go society will follow', he confidently predicted and he was soon proved right; today Leinster House is used as the Irish Parliament and is in the epicentre of Georgian Dublin. This area has museums, fine houses, landscaped squares and some of the best restaurants in the city.

GEORGIAN DUBLIN

🅒 SEE

🅒 SHOP

🍴 EAT

🍸 DRINK

⭐ PLAY

Please see over for map

SEE

FITZWILLIAM SQUARE

🚌 10, 11, 13b, 46a, 5

The smallest and last of Dublin's great Georgian squares, Fitzwilliam is home to a quiet and elegant block of immaculate terraces, boasting some elaborate doors and fanlights. While by day the square houses doctors' surgeries and solicitors' offices, by night prostitutes await custom. Only residents have access to the central garden.

GOVERNMENT BUILDINGS

☎ 662 4888; www.taoiseach.gov .ie; Upper Merrion St; admission free, tickets available from National Gallery on day of visit; 🕑 10.30am-3.30pm Sat; 🚌 7, 7a, 8, 45; 🚉 Pearse; 🚹 by arrangement

The domed Government Buildings, constructed in an Edwardian interpretation of the Georgian style, were opened originally in 1911 as the Royal College of Science. Tours lasting around 40 minutes include the new wing, renovated in the 1990s at a whopping cost of €17.4 million, with the Taoiseach's office and the ceremonial staircase. The much more atmospheric old wing houses the cabinet room where Irish Free State ministers met for the first time.

BY GEORGE

The Georgian period is roughly defined as the years between the accession of George I in 1714 and the death of George IV in 1830. Its inspiration was the work of the 16th-century Italian architect Andrea Palladio, who believed reason and the principles of classical antiquity should govern building.

In Dublin, the austere formality of the style was tempered by the use of coloured doors, delicate fanlights, intricate ironwork and exuberant interior plasterwork.

IRISH-JEWISH MUSEUM

☎ 490 1857; 3-4 Walworth Rd; admission free; 🕑 11am-3.30pm Tue, Thu & Sun May-Sep, 10.30am-2.30pm Sun Oct-Apr; 🚌 14, 15, 16, 19, 83, 122; 🚹 limited

Dublin's dwindling Jewish population is remembered through photographs, paintings, certificates, books and other memorabilia in this terrace house in the former Jewish district of Portobello. The museum re-creates a typical 19th-century Dublin kosher kitchen, while upstairs is an old synagogue, in a state of disuse since the 1970s.

IVEAGH GARDENS

☎ 475 7816; www.heritageireland.ie; Clonmel St; admission free; 🕑 8am-dusk Mon-Sat, from 10am Sun; 🚌 14, 14a, 15a, 15b; 🚉 Harcourt; 🚹 good

Once known to locals as the Secret Garden, the word is now out about

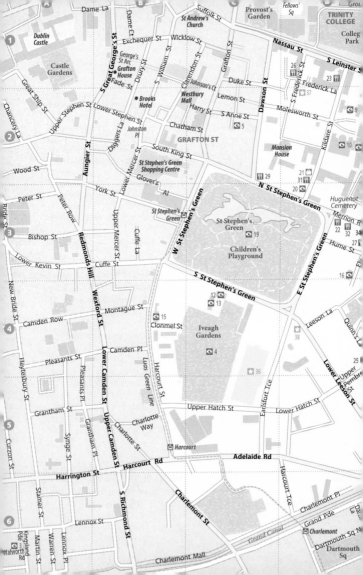

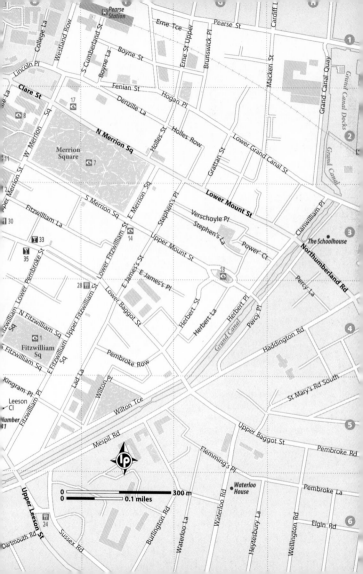

Reading room, National Library

the beautiful and ramshackle Iveagh Gardens, situated just behind Newman House. Accessible from either Earlsfort Tce or Harcourt St, and less crowded than nearby St Stephen's Green, the gardens were designed by Ninian Niven in 1863. Features of the beautifully landscaped gardens include a wonderfully rustic grotto, cascade, fountain, maze and rose garden.

KERLIN GALLERY

☎ 670 9093; www.kerlin.ie; Anne's Lane, S Anne St; admission free; ✆ 10am-5.45pm Mon-Fri, 11am-4.30pm Sat; 🚌 10, 14, 14a, 15

Hidden behind a nondescript door in a dingy little lane, the Kerlin Gallery is the ultimate statement in cool. Inside, the minimalist space displays mainly conceptual and abstract art from some of Ireland's leading lights, including Sean Scully and Jaki Irvine.

◪ LEINSTER HOUSE

☎ 618 3000, tour info 618 3271; www .oireachtas.ie; Kildare St; admission free; ◷ public gallery open when parliament in session, usually Nov–May; ▣ 7, 7a, 8, 10, 11, 13; ▣ Pearse Station; ♿ good

The Dáil and Seanad both meet at Leinster House, Ireland's parliament, when it sits for 90 days every year. Designed by Richard Cassels for the duke of Leinster, the Kildare St frontage is intended to look like a town house, while from Merrion St it appears to look like a country estate. The White House in the United States, designed by Irish architect James Hoban, was allegedly modelled on its design.

◪ MERRION SQUARE

▣ 5, 7, 7a, 8, 45; ▣ Pearse Station; ♿ good

Merrion Square is lined with stately Georgian buildings whose doors, peacock fanlights, ornate door knockers and foot-scrapers epitomise the elegance of the era. Former residents include the Wilde family, WB Yeats and Daniel O'Connell. Its lush central gardens are perfect for a picnic or peaceful pit stop.

NATIONAL GALLERY UNMISSABLES

> *The Liffey Swim*, Jack B Yeats
> *Lady Writing a Letter*, Vermeer
> *The Cottage Girl*, Gainsborough
> *Still Life with Mandolin*, Picasso

◪ NATIONAL GALLERY OF IRELAND

☎ 661 5133; www.nationalgallery.ie; W Merrion Sq; admission free; 9.30am–5.30pm Mon–Wed, Fri & Sat, to 8.30pm Thu, noon–5.30pm Sun, free guided tours 3pm Sat, 2pm, 3pm & 4pm Sun, 3pm daily Jul & Aug, public lectures 10.30am Tue, 3pm Sun; ▣ 5, 7, 7a, 10, 13a, 44c, 48a; ▣ Pearse Station; ♿ excellent

The collection at the National Gallery is made up of nearly 13,000 paintings, sketches, prints and sculptures, including such highlights as Caravaggio's *The Taking of Christ* and the impressive Beit Collection, made up of a huge collection of masterpieces by Vermeer, Velázquez and Goya. Our favourites, however, are the paintings of William's brother Jack B Yeats.

◪ NATIONAL LIBRARY

☎ 603 0200; www.nli.ie; Kildare St; admission through free ticket; ◷ 10am–9pm Mon–Wed, to 5pm Thu–Fri, to 1pm Sat; ▣ 10, 11, 13; ♿ limited

Soak up the atmosphere of the library's gorgeous domed reading

 JAMES HANLEY RHA
Painter

The National Gallery has been a part of my life since I was a small boy and first came across Nathaniel Hone's *Pasture at Malahide*. It and the rest of the collection have been seared into my consciousness ever since – I remember once standing in front of an El Greco and realising that he too once stood three feet from the painting, as I was doing.

Another nice memory was from my student days, when I was giving a tour and we stopped in front of Murillo's six panels telling the story of the Prodigal Son. Like the subject in the painting, I too had a hole in my shoe; a woman asked for my shoe size and a few weeks' later I received a brand new pair of shoes in the post!

I am immensely proud of the gallery, and proud that in 2003 I finally realised my dream and saw one of room (mentioned in Joyce's *Ulysses*). The extensive collection includes early manuscripts, first editions, maps and other items of interest. A major exhibition on WB Yeats will run until 2009 and temporary exhibitions are often held on the ground floor. On the 2nd floor is the Genealogical Office.

NATIONAL MUSEUM OF IRELAND – ARCHAEOLOGY & HISTORY

☎ 677 7444; www.museum.ie; Kildare St; admission free, guided tours €2; 🕒 10am-5pm Tue-Sat, 2-5pm Sun, regular guided tours 2-5pm; 🚌 7, 7a, 10, 25x, 39x, 51d, 51x; 🚆 Pearse Station; ♿ limited

Inside the Palladian-style National Museum, with its massive domed rotunda, classical marble columns and ornate mosaic ceilings and floors, you'll find a bounty of Bronze Age gold, Iron Age Celtic metalwork, Viking artefacts and ancient Egyptian relics. Call ahead for family programmes on weekends.

NATIONAL MUSEUM OF IRELAND – NATURAL HISTORY

☎ 677 7444; www.museum.ie; Merrion St; admission free; 🕒 10am-5pm Tue-Sat, from 2pm Sun; 🚌 7, 7a; ♿ limited

Scarcely changed since 1857, this terrifically antiquated place unashamedly eschews the 21st

> **NATIONAL MUSEUM MUST SEES**
> > Broighter Hoard
> > Cross of Cong
> > Lurgan Logboat
> > *Ten Years Collecting* exhibit

century with its dusty dinosaur-era displays and authentic Victorian atmosphere. The creaking interior gives way to an overwhelming display of stuffed animals and mounted heads, crammed in like something from a Hitchcock movie. Of the two million species on display here, many are long extinct.

NEWMAN HOUSE

☎ 706 7422; 85-86 S St Stephen's Green; admission €5/4; 🕒 by guided tour noon, 2pm, 3pm & 4pm Tue-Fri Jun-Sep; 🚌 10, 11, 13, 14, 15a; 🚆 St Stephen's Green

Part of University College Dublin, Newman House consists of two exquisitely restored Georgian town houses with spectacular 18th-century stucco interiors. Don't miss the Apollo Room and the Saloon by Paulo and Filipo LaFranchini, and later work by Robert West. Former students of Newman House include writer James Joyce and former president Eamon de Valera.

☉ NEWMAN UNIVERSITY CHURCH

☎ 478 0616; 83 S St Stephen's Green; admission free; ☉ 8am-6pm Mon-Sat; 🚌 10, 11, 13, 14, 14a, 15a, 15b
This Catholic church was built between 1854 and 1856 in an elaborate Byzantine style with multicoloured marble and copious gold leaf, making it very fashionable for society weddings. Cardinal Newman, who founded the city's first Catholic university next door at Newman House, is honoured with a bust.

☉ NUMBER 29

☎ 702 6165; www.esb.ie; 29 Lower Fitzwilliam St; admission €4.50/2, under 16 free; ☉ 10am-5pm Tue-Sat, from 1pm Sun; 🚌 6, 7, 10, 45; 🚉 Pearse Station
Built in 1794 for the widow of a wine merchant, Number 29 reconstructs genteel Dublin home life from 1790 to 1820. Discover how Georgians bathed twice yearly and how ladies used a latter-day mini gym, the leather exercise horse. See the discreet dining-room mirrors that allowed servants to respond to orders without listening in to round-table gossip. The 30-minute tour is a fascinating taste of the city's social history.

☉ ORIGIN GALLERY

☎ 478 5159; 83 Harcourt St; admission free; ☉ 10.30am-5.30pm Mon-Fri, noon-4pm Sat; 🚌 14, 15, 16, 19; 🚉 Harcourt
A relaxed space on the 1st floor of a Georgian terrace, Origin functions primarily as a showcase for artists who've stayed at the gallery's County Kerry retreat, Cill Rialaig, and emerging artists putting on their first show. In a similarly encouraging spirit, buyers can pay in installments.

☉ RHA GALLAGHER GALLERY

☎ 661 2558; www.royalhibernicacademy.com; 25 Ely Pl; admission free; ☉ 11am-5pm Tue-Sat, from 2pm Sun; 🚌 10, 11, 13b, 51x; ♿ excellent
Established in 1823, the Royal Hibernian Academy has four galleries

MUSIC OF THE GODS

Many of Dublin's churches have accomplished choirs that make full use of the heavenly acoustics.
> Christ Church Cathedral (p99) Come to hear choral evensong four times a week (call for more information).
> St Patrick's Cathedral (p105) Hear the choir sing evensong and try to book tickets for the carols performed around Christmas.
> St Stephen's Church (opposite) The acoustics in the 'Peppercanister Church' are superb. It hosts concerts on an ad hoc basis.

in a large impressive modernist space; three are dedicated to curated exhibits featuring a wide range of Irish and international visual art; the Ashford Gallery promotes the work of Academy members and artists who haven't yet secured commercial representation.

☉ ROYAL INSTITUTE OF ARCHITECTS OF IRELAND

☎ 676 1703; www.riai.ie; 8 N Merrion Sq; admission free; ☿ 9.30am-5pm Mon-Fri; 🚌 5, 7, 27x, 44, 45; ♿ good

The gallery at this headquarters is host to specialist exhibitions that will excite anyone with an interest in building design. Irish and international shows have ranged in topic from ethnic minority architecture to Irish footpaths. The institute's own awards show reflects the changing face of Irish building.

☉ ST STEPHEN'S CHURCH

☎ 288 0663; Mount St Cres; admission free; ☿ services only, 11am Sun; 🚌 5, 7, 7a, 8, 45, 46; 🚊 Grand Canal Dock

Built in 1825 in Greek Revival style, St Stephen's is commonly known as the 'Peppercanister Church' because of its shape. It hosts classical concerts from time to time.

☉ ST STEPHEN'S GREEN

admission free; ☿ 8am-dusk Mon-Sat; 🚊 Pearse Station; 🚊 St Stephen's Green; ♿ good

St Stephen's Green bandstand

Once a common where public whippings, burnings and hangings took place, the 9 hectares of St Stephen's Green now provide

NEIGHBOURHOODS

GEORGIAN DUBLIN

a popular lunchtime escape for city workers. Geese, ducks and waterfowl splash about the ponds, there's a good children's play-ground and the bandstand hosts concerts in summer. From 10am Sunday, Garden for the Blind has Braille signs and plants that can be handled. See also p16.

TAYLOR GALLERIES

☎ 676 6055; 16 Kildare St; admission free; 🕙 10am-5.30pm Mon-Fri, 11am-3pm Sat; 🚌 10, 11, 13; 🚇 Pearse Station; 🚻 good

Founded in 1978, Taylor Galleries is the original of the pack. Housed in a fine Georgian building, it shows Ireland's top contemporary artists like Louis le Brocquy, Patrick Scott, Tony O'Malley and Brian Bourke to a well-heeled clientele.

🛍 SHOP

🛍 MITCHELL & SON WINE MERCHANTS

☎ 676 0766; 21 Kildare St; 🕙 9am-5.30pm Mon-Fri, from 10.30am Sat; 🚌 11, 11a, 14, 14a, 15a; 🚇 St Stephen's Green

Established in 1805, the store is still run by a sixth- and seventh-generation Mitchell father-and-son team. Wines, champagnes, Irish whiskey and Cuban cigars fill the cavernous space. You can also buy stylish wine racks, glasses, hip flasks and ice buckets.

EAT

🍴 BANG CAFÉ

Modern European   €€€

☎ 676 0898; 11 Merrion Row; 🕙 12.30-3pm & 6-10.30pm Mon-Wed, to 11pm Thu-Sat; 🚌 10, 11, 13b, 51; 🚻 V

One of our favourite restaurants in Dublin, Bang Café justifi-ably earned a Bib Gourmand (good food at moderate prices) from those Michelin folks. Chef Lorcan Cribbin whips up a diverse menu that includes roast squab pigeon and gorgeous John Dory with langoustines. Don't leave without trying the heavenly warm chocolate brownie, oozing with chocolate sauce. The atmosphere is young, vibrant and eternally stylish.

🍴 CAIFÉ UNA *Café*   €€

☎ 670 6087; 46 Kildare St; 🕙 noon-6pm Mon-Sat, 6-9.30pm Tue-Sat; 🚇 St Stephen's Green; 🚻 V

You don't have to speak the lingo to appreciate this earthy yet chic little Irish-language café. Its basement walls are covered in contemporary art and – in a nice touch – the handwritten work of Irish poets. The food is good modern Irish with favourites such as stew, pea and mint soup and marinated lamb shoulder featuring.

🍴 CANAL BANK CAFÉ
Bistro   €€€

☎ 664 2135; 146 Upper Leeson St;
🕙 10am-11pm, from 11am Sat & Sun;
🚌 11, 46, 118; 🚹 Ⓥ

Life is good at Trevor Browne's airy American-French–style bistro, just off the canal. Make a big lunch date with black sole on the bone, fragrant lobster and fantastic Brooklyn meatloaf – prices are the same, day and evening.

🍴 DAX *French/European*   €€€

☎ 676 1494; 23 Upper Pembroke St;
🕙 noon-2.15pm Tue-Fri, 6-11pm Tue-Sat; 🚌 10, 11, 46b; 🚹

Olivier Meisonnave, convivial ex–maître d of Thornton's stepped out on his own with Irish chef Pól Óhéannraich to open this posh, rustic restaurant named after his home town, north of Biarritz. Located in a bright basement, serious foodies can sate their palate on sea bass with celeriac purée, pork wrapped in serrano ham or truffle risotto.

🍴 DUNNE & CRESCENZI
Italian wine bar   €

☎ 675 9892; 14 & 16 S Frederick St;
🕙 8.30am-11pm Mon-Sat, noon-6pm Sun; 🚌 all cross-city; 🚹 Ⓥ

People know a good thing when they see it. The folks from Bar Italia (p73) do it in style again this side of town and the crowds keep

coming. Take your pick from a choice of two daily pastas, antipasti and bruschetta dripping in fruity olive oil, and a selection of eminently drinkable Italian wines.

🍴 ELY *Organic*   €€€

☎ 676 8986; 22 Ely Pl; 🕙 noon-3pm Mon-Fri, 1-4pm Sat, 6-9.30pm Mon-Wed, to 10.30pm Thu-Sat 🚌 10, 15; 🚹 Ⓥ

Scrummy homemade burgers, bangers and mash or wild smoked salmon salad are some of what you'll find in this basement restaurant. Dishes are prepared with organic and free-range produce from the owner's family farm in County Clare, so you can rest assured of the quality. There's a large wine list to choose from, with more than 70 sold by the glass. Now with a big new branch at the atmospheric old tobacco warehouse CHQ building in the **IFSC** (☎ 672 0010; Hanover Quay).

🍴 L'ECRIVAIN
French/Irish   €€€€

☎ 661 1919; www.lecrivain.com; 112 Lower Baggot St; 🕙 12.30-2pm Mon-Fri, 7-11pm Mon-Sat; 🚌 10, 11, 13b, 51; 🚹 Ⓥ

Many foodies consider this the best restaurant in town, and the recent acquisition of a second Michelin star points that way. Heaven-made combinations of the best local, seasonal produce –

wild salmon, Dublin Bay prawns, veal and Barbary duck – are matched with inventive sauces and accompaniments and presented like works of art. An attentive but friendly staff makes for a dining experience that is far from stuffy.

🍴 PEPLOES European €€€
☎ 676 3144; 16 N St Stephen's Green; ⏰ noon-11pm; 🚌 all cross-city; 🚊 St Stephen's Green; ♿ Ⓥ

The buzz that surrounded the opening of Barry Canny's Peploes in 2003 has hardly abated. Great-value comfort dishes such as rabbit cassoulet with gnocchi or half a dozen Carlingford oysters keep the mainly business crowd happy, but it's the loud, conspiratorial atmosphere in the former bank vault that keeps 'em coming back.

🍴 RESTAURANT PATRICK GUILBAUD French €€€€
☎ 676 4192; 21 Upper Merrion St; ⏰ 12.30-2.15pm & 7.30-10.15pm Tue-Sat; 🚌 all cross-city; ♿ ♿ Ⓥ

This elegant restaurant (two Michelin stars) is one of the country's finest. Service is formal and faultless, chef Guillaume Lebrun's food is proudly French and the wine list is extensive. Surprisingly, the dishes here are not overly fussy; it's just excellent produce, beautifully cooked and well presented.

🍴 TOWN BAR & GRILL
Modern Italian €€€
☎ 662 4724; 21 Kildare St; ⏰ noon-11pm, to 10pm Sun ; 🚌 10, 11, 15; 🚊 St Stephen's Green; ♿ Ⓥ

Though its menu is quintes-sentially Italian, the last thing you'll find on this menu is pizza margherita or spag bol. This cool basement trattoria serves chic upmarket Italian fare that you'd more likely come across in down-town New York, such as a solvent, swanky set feast on crayfish bisque, slow-roasted rabbit and feta and sweet pepper-stuffed lamb.

🍴 UNICORN *Italian* €€€
☎ 676 2182; 12b Merrion Ct, Merrion Row; ⏰ 12.30-3.30pm & 6-11.30pm Mon-Sat; 🚌 10, 11, 13b, 51x; ♿ ♿ Ⓥ

Saturday lunch at the fashion-able Unicorn has been a noisy Dublin tradition for over half a century, as media types, politicos and legal eagles gossip and clink glasses in conspiratorial rapture. At lunch many opt for the anti-pasto bar, while the bistro-style evening menu features Italian classics.

DRINK
DOHENY & NESBITT'S

☎ 676 2945; 5 Lower Baggot St; 🚌 10, 11, 13b, 51x; 🚇 to 7pm

Opened in 1867 as a grocer's shop, this pub has antique snugs, dark-wood panelling and a pressed-metal roof. It's a favourite haunt of politicians and journalists, Leinster House (p57) being just a short stroll away.

O'DONOGHUE'S

☎ 676 2807; 15 Merrion Row; 🚌 10, 11, 13b, 51x; 🚇 to 7pm

O'Donoghue's is the most renowned traditional music bar in Dublin, where well-known folk group the Dubliners started out in the 1960s. On warm summer evenings a young, international crowd spills into the courtyard beside the pub.

TONER'S

☎ 676 3090; 139 Lower Baggot St; 🚌 10, 11, 13b, 51x; 🚇 to 7pm

With its stone floor and old grocer's shelves and drawers, Toner's feels like a country pub in the heart of the city. Though Victorian, it's not elaborate and draws a crowd of mainly businessmen and hacks. It's not touristy but many visitors seek out its simple charms.

★ PLAY
NATIONAL CONCERT HALL

☎ bookings 417 0000, info 417 0077; www.nch.ie; Earlsfort Tce; 🕙 box office 10am-7pm Mon-Sat; 🚌 10, 11, 13, 14, 15, 44, 86; 🚇 Harcourt; 🚻 good; 🚼 special summer concerts

Ireland's premier classical concert venue hosts performances by the National Symphony Orchestra and international artists, as well as jazz, traditional Irish and contemporary concerts. From June to September it has inexpensive concerts on Tuesday from 1.05pm to 2pm.

RENARD'S

☎ 677 5876; www.renards.ie; S Frederick St; admission free-€10; 🕙 10.30pm-2.30am; 🚌 all cross-city

Run by Colin Farrell's godfather and his (and other celebs) favourite den of iniquity when in town, Renard's is an intimate club with a strict door policy when busy. Music is mainly house, with soul, funk and jazz making the odd appearance.

SUGAR CLUB

☎ 678 7188; 8 Lower Leeson St; admission €8-20; 🕙 8.30pm; 🚌 11, 46, 118

Sink into big banquette seats with a cocktail served on the spot as you absorb up-and-coming jazz, folk, rock, indie and comedy acts in one of Dublin's most comfortable and stylish venues.

>TEMPLE BAR

Temple Bar gets its fair share of bad press. And some would say justifiably so. There's no denying with a bar on every corner (and some in between), it has earned its reputation as Europe's premier stomping ground for raucous, bawdy hen and stag parties. For the legions of revellers who don their themed T-shirts and reveal-all outfits ready for a night of drinking, laughing and scoring, Temple Bar is the best part of the Dublin experience; for those looking for a more cultural, authentic insight into the capital, Temple Bar is a high-octane cheesefest, artificially manufactured to clean out unsuspecting wallets. That said, the city's prime entertainment and eating spot still has a tangible history and atmosphere that you can't help but feel as you walk its narrow, medieval cobbled streets.

TEMPLE BAR

◉ SEE
City Hall 1 B4
Contemporary
Music Centre 2 A4
Cultivate 3 A4
Gallery of Photography.. 4 B3
National Photographic
Archives 5 B3
Original Print Gallery 6 C3
Sunlight Chambers 7 B3
Temple Bar
Gallery & Studios............ 8 C3

⌂ SHOP
5 Scarlett Row 9 A4
Anthology 10 B4
Claddagh Records 11 C3
Cow's Lane Market........ 12 A4
DesignYard .... (see 12)
Flip................................... 13 C4

Forbidden Planet 14 C3
Haus................................. 15 C4
Meeting House
Square Market............... 16 B3
Retrospect...................... 17 A4
Rhythm Records 18 C3
Smock............................. 19 A4
Urban Outfitters 20 C3

▥ EAT
Bar Italia 21 A3
Chameleon 22 C3
Eden 23 B3
Elephant & Castle.......... 24 C3
Gruel............................... 25 B4
Larder 26 B4
Mermaid Café................ 27 B4
Monty's of
Kathmandu 28 C4
Queen of Tarts 29 B4
Tea Rooms 30 B3

▾ DRINK
Octagon Bar 31 B3
Oliver St John
Gogarty's 32 D3
Palace Bar...................... 33 D3
Porterhouse Brewing
Company 34 B3

★ PLAY
Boilerhouse Sauna 35 B4
Ha'penny Bridge Inn 36 C4
Hub 37 C4
Irish Film Institute 38 B4
Mezz 39 C4
Olympia Theatre 40 B4
Project Arts Centre........ 41 B3
Rogue 42 B4
Temple Bar
Music Centre.................. 43 C3

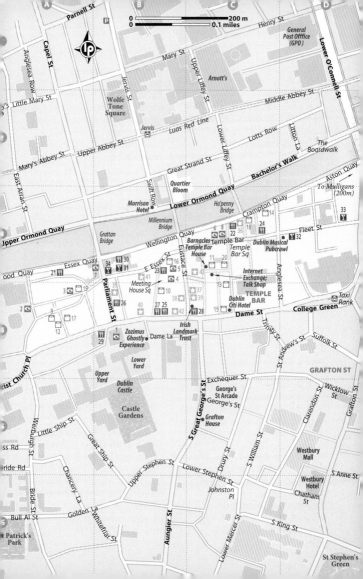

◉ SEE

◉ CITY HALL

☎ 672 2204; Cork Hill, Dame St; admission €4/2/10; ☽ 10am-5.15pm Mon-Sat, 2-5pm Sun; ◻ 50, 50a, 54, 56a, 77, 77a, 123, 150; ♿ excellent

Restored to its Georgian glory, City Hall is adorned with neoclassical columns, a domed, gilded rotunda and patterned marble floors. Built by Thomas Cooley as the Royal Exchange from 1769 to 1779, the funerals of Michael Collins and Charles Stewart Parnell were held here. The *Story of the Capital* exhibition in the arched vaults traces Dublin's history with artefacts, models and multimedia displays.

◉ CONTEMPORARY MUSIC CENTRE

☎ 490 1857; www.cmc.ie; 19 Fishamble St; admission free; ☽ 10am-5.30pm Mon-Fri; ◻ all city-centre; ♿ limited

Anyone with an interest in Irish contemporary music must visit the national archive here where you can hear (and play around with on an electronic organ) 5000 samples from composers of this and the last century. There's a good reference library where you can attend courses and meet composers.

◉ CULTIVATE

☎ 674 5773; www.sustainable.ie; 15-19 W Essex St; admission free; ☽ 10am-5.30pm Mon-Sat; ◻ all cross-city

Dublin's sustainable living and learning centre is a one-stop shop for all you ever wanted to know about eco-living. As well as selling everything from electric bikes to wood pellet stoves, it organises workshops and slow food brunches.

◉ GALLERY OF PHOTOGRAPHY

☎ 671 4654; www.irish-photography .com; Meeting House Sq; admission free; ☽ 11am-6pm Tue-Sat, from 1pm Sun; ◻ all city-centre; ♿ good

Ireland's premier photographic gallery, this place has ever-changing exhibits, often with Irish themes. Directly across the square you'll find the **National Photographic Archive** (☎ 603 0371; ☽ 10am-5pm Mon-Fri, to 2pm Sat), which displays predominantly historical photographs from the National Library's collection.

◉ ORIGINAL PRINT GALLERY

☎ 677 3657; www.originalprint.ie; 4 Temple Bar; admission free; ☽ 10.30am-5.30pm Mon-Fri, 11am-5pm Sat, 2-6pm Sun; ◻ all city-centre; ◻ Tara Street

The gallery's back catalogue of work from 150 Irish and international printmakers is available for purchase, along with new, limited-edition work. It's a great place to browse for pressies (yes, for yourself too), many starting at under €100, among the diverse range of prints on display.

 SUNLIGHT CHAMBERS

Essex Quay; 🚌 **all city-centre**

Sunlight Chambers, on the southern banks of the Liffey, stands out among the Georgian and modern architecture for its beautiful Art Nouveau friezework. Sunlight was a brand of soap made by Lever Brothers. The frieze shows the Lever Brothers' view of the world: men make clothes dirty, women wash them.

TEMPLE BAR GALLERY & STUDIOS

☎ **671 0073; www.templebargallery .com; 5-9 Temple Bar;** 🕐 **11am-6pm Tue, Wed, Fri & Sat, to 7pm Thu;** 🚌 **all city-centre;** 🚆 **Tara Street;** ♿ **good**

TBG has contemporary, thoughtful shows in a variety of media from a broad range of local and international artists. Set up in 1983 as an artist-run space, the gallery provides affordable studios and shows interesting shows from emerging painters, sculptors and mixed-media artists.

SHOP

5 SCARLET ROW

☎ **672 9534; 5 Scarlet Row, W Essex St;** 🕐 **11am-6pm Mon-Sat;** 🚌 **all cross-city**

Beautiful, modern, exclusive, minimalist. If that's what you're after

Crown Alley near Temple Bar

try the creations of Eley Kishimoto, Zero, Irish designer Sharon Wauchob or menswear label Unis. Co-owner Eileen Shields worked with Donna Karan in New York before returning to Dublin to found her own gorgeous shoe label which retails here.

ANTHOLOGY

☎ 635 1422; Meeting House Sq; ⏱ 10am-9pm Tue-Sat, noon-6pm Sun; 🚊 Jervis

A bright artsy bookshop selling beautiful books and DVDs on design, film, poetry, philosophy and politics, it also holds writing-related courses and workshops. There's an inspired children's section here too.

CLADDAGH RECORDS

☎ 677 0262; 2 Cecilia St; ⏱ 10.30am-5.30pm Mon-Fri, from noon Sat; 🚊 all cross-city; 🚊 Jervis

An intimate, well-loved shop with knowledgeable staff, Claddagh specialises in folk, traditional and ethnic music from Ireland, the USA and South America.

COW'S LANE MARKET

Cow's Lane; ⏱ 10am-5pm Sat; 🚊 all cross-city; 🚊 Jervis

A real market for hipsters, this market brings together more than 60 of the best clothing, accessory and craft stalls in town. Buy punky T-shirts, retro handbags, cutting-edge designer duds from the likes of Drunk Monk, costume jewellery by Kink Bijoux, and even clubby baby wear.

DESIGNYARD

☎ 474 1011; Cow's Lane; ⏱ 9.30am-6.30pm Mon-Wed & Fri, to 8pm Thu, 9am-6.30pm Sat, 10am-6pm Sun; 🚊 all cross-city

A high-end, craft-as-art shop where everything you see – glass, batik, sculpture, painting – is one-off and handmade in Ireland. It also showcases contemporary jewellery stock from young international designers.

FLIP

☎ 671 4299; 4 Fownes St; ⏱ 10am-6pm Mon-Wed & Fri, to 7pm Thu & Sat, 1.30-6pm Sun; 🚊 all cross-city; 🚊 St Stephen's Green

This hip Irish label takes the best male fashion moods of the 1950s and serves them back to us, minus the mothball smell. US college shirts, logo T-shirts, Oriental and Hawaiian shirts, Fonz-style leather jackets and well-cut jeans mix it with the genuine second-hand gear upstairs.

FORBIDDEN PLANET

☎ 671 0688; 5-6 Crampton Quay; ⏱ 10am-7pm Mon-Wed & Fri, to 8pm Thu, to 6pm Sat, 11am-4pm Sun; 🚊 all cross-city; 🚊 Abbey Street

Science-fiction and fantasy specialist, with books, videos, comics, magazines, figurines and posters. Just the place for those Dr Spock ears or a *Star Wars* light sabre.

HANDEL WITH CARE

In 1742 the nearly broke GF Handel conducted the very first performance of his epic work *Messiah* in the since-demolished Dublin Music Hall, on the city's oldest street, Fishamble St. Ironically, Jonathan Swift – author of *Gulliver's Travels* and dean of St Patrick's Cathedral – having suggested his own and Christchurch's choir participate, revoked his invitation, vowing to 'punish such vicars for their rebellion, disobedience and perfidy'. The concert went ahead nonetheless, and the celebrated work is now performed at the original spot in Dublin annually.

☐ HAUS

☎ 679 5155; 3-4 Crow St; ⏱ 9am-6pm Mon-Fri, from 10am Sat; 🚌 all cross-city
Cutting-edge designer furniture and homewares from the drawing boards of the big names, such as Phillipe Starck, Le Corbusier and Ireland's own Eileen Gray.

☐ MEETING HOUSE SQUARE MARKET

Meeting House Sq; ⏱ 9am-5pm Sat; 🚌 all cross-city; 🚆 Jervis
One of the best places to spend Saturday morning, this market buzzes with visitors and locals stocking up on organic, gourmet and imported exotica. Munch on sushi, paella, waffles, crepes and sizzling sausages, while perusing stalls of farmhouse cheeses, hand-pressed juices, organic meats and tubs of garlic pesto.

☐ RETROSPECT

☎ 672 6188; 2 Cow's Lane; ⏱ 11.30am-6.30pm Mon, Fri & Sat, to 5pm Wed, to 7pm Thu, 11am-4pm Sun; 🚌 all cross-city
All you children of the 1960s and '70s can relive the era that taste forgot (or took off, depending on your viewpoint) at this vintage interiors shop. In here you'll discover fantastic plastic objects of desire, formica-top tables, original lava lamps and swinging egg seats, all of them in glorious technicolours.

☐ RHYTHM RECORDS

☎ 671 9594; 1 Aston Quay; ⏱ 11am-6pm Mon-Sat; 🚌 all cross-city; 🚆 Abbey Street
This grungy little store on the quays has a large U2 section, including major releases, singles, special tour editions, remix albums and suspicious-looking cassettes with photocopied covers. Also posters, videos, postcards and 7-inchers.

☐ SMOCK

☎ 613 9000; Smock Alley Ct, W Essex St; ⏱ 10.30am-6pm Mon-Fri, 10am-6pm Sat; 🚌 all cross-city
This tiny designer shop on the edge of Temple Bar features

Leigh Tucker
Designer, Leighlee

If you're a woman, shopping in Dublin is fantastic; for its size, it has a range of diversity comparable with any of the cities you'd associate with great retail, including London, Paris and New York. If you're a man, and aren't a skateboarder or a middle-aged business type, then you're in trouble, for there is very little to choose from.

My favourite boutique in Dublin is Smock. It has all of the clothes I'd like in my wardrobe. It's quite unique in the city; it takes risks in the stock it buys, and generally those risks pay off. It's not for everyday Irish women — the prices ensure that — but it has a strong, loyal customer base that keeps it going. It may be part of the family business, but Costume (p84) *is* another fabulous shop. They stock lots of exclusive labels that are hard to find, they steer clear of generic department store buying…and they stock my clothes!

cutting-edge international women's wear from classy 'investment labels' such as Easton Pearson, Veronique Branquinho and AF Vandevorft, as well as a small range of interesting jewellery and lingerie.

URBAN OUTFITTERS

☎ 670 6202; 7 Fownes St; ⏰ 10am-7pm Mon-Wed & Fri, to 8pm Thu & Sat, 11am-6pm Sun; 🚌 all cross-city

Funky street wear and labels are mixed with gadgets and homewares at this branch of the US chain. As the DJ spins tunes from the Carbon record outlet, boys browse through G-Star denims, Pringle knits and Fiorucci trousers, while girls have a choice between Claudie Pierlot, W&LT and Mandarina Duck.

🍴 EAT

🍴 BAR ITALIA *Italian* €

☎ 679 5128; Unit 4, The Bookend, Essex Quay; ⏰ 8am-5pm Mon-Wed, to 6pm Thu & Fri, 9am-6pm Sat; 🚌 all cross-city 🚻 Ⓥ

This place is tiny, noisy and you have to queue up with the barristers from the Four Courts across the river for a table, but we absolutely love Bar Italia. Perhaps it's the fantastic Palombini coffee, the rich chocolate tart or the scrummy daily pastas. Probably though it's the constant buzz of the Italian waitstaff, whizzing between the tables in their frantic, friendly way.

🍴 CHAMELEON *Indonesian* €€

☎ 671 0362; 1 Lower Fownes St; ⏰ 6-11pm Tue-Sat, to 10pm Sun; 🚌 all cross-city; 🚻 Ⓥ

Friendly, characterful and draped in exotic fabrics, Chameleon serves up oodles of noodles and Indonesian classics such as satay, *gado gado* (veggies with peanut sauce), *nasi goreng* (fried rice) and *mee goreng* (spicy fried noodles). If you simply cannot make up your mind, try the *rijsttafel* – a selection of several dishes served with rice.

🍴 EDEN *Modern Irish* €€€

☎ 670 5372; Meeting House Sq; ⏰ noon-3pm & 6-10.30pm, to 11pm Sat & Sun; 🚌 all cross-city; 🚻 Ⓥ

Reminiscent of a swimming pool, with its aquamarine mosaic walls and ceiling-to-floor windows onto Meeting House Sq, Eden's minimalist surroundings belie Eleanor Walsh's wonderful, organic seasonal menu that brings the best of Irish produce to your table. Roast sea bass with *salsa verde* (spicy green sauce) and couscous or beef in Guinness are clear winners with its glitteringly hip patrons.

FOOD ON THE FLY

Need some fuel in a hurry? These places offer great food with quick service or a takeaway option.

> Bar Italia (p73)
> Gruel (below)
> Panem (p117)
> Fallon & Byrne – downstairs (p90)
> Simon's Place (p92)

🍴 ELEPHANT & CASTLE
American €€

☎ 679 3121; 18 Temple Bar; 🕒 8am-11.30pm Mon-Fri, 11.30am-11.30pm Sat & Sun; 🚌 all cross-city; 🧖 V

If it's massive New York–style sandwiches or sticky chicken wings you're after, this bustling upmarket diner is just the joint. Be prepared to queue though, especially at weekends when Elephant & Castle heaves with the hassled parents of wandering toddlers, wealthy suburbanites and hungover 20-somethings, all in pursuit of a carb-fest and quiet corner to peruse the paper.

🍴 GRUEL *Modern European* €€

☎ 670 7119; 68a Dame St; 🕒 7am-9.30pm Mon-Fri, 10.30am-4pm Sat & Sun 🚌 all cross-city; 🧖 V

Run by the excellent Mermaid Café (right) crew, Gruel offers more sophisticated food than its name suggests. The atmosphere may be relaxed New York–style caff with walls covered in gig posters, but the food is dead serious. Expect slow roast meats or vegetables in crusty bread, zinging salads, baked fish or its trademark bangers and mash in the evening.

🍴 LARDER *Café* €

☎ 633 3581; 8 Parliament St; 🕒 7.30am-5.30pm Mon-Fri, from 9am Sat; 🚌 7b, 11, 121; 🧖 V

This new café has an organic vibe to it, what with its wholesome porridge breakfasts, gourmet sandwiches such as serrano ham, gruyere and rocket and Japanese speciality *suki* teas (try the China gunpowder). It's confident about its food – we like the fact that it lists suppliers – and so are we.

🍴 MERMAID CAFÉ
Modern European €€€

☎ 670 8236; 69 Dame St; 🕒 12.30-2.30pm & 6-11pm Mon-Sat, 12.30-3pm & 6-9pm Sun; 🚌 all cross-city; 🧖 V

This French-American–style bistro with elemental furniture and sparse artwork on its walls caters to a hip gourmand crowd who appreciate inventive ingredient-led, organic food such as New England crab cakes, mouth-watering steaks or robust cassoulets. The informal atmosphere, pure food and friendly staff make it difficult to get a table without a prior reservation.

🍴 MONTY'S OF KATHMANDU
Nepalese €€

☎ 670 4911; 28 Eustace St ; ⏲ 12.30-2.30pm & 6-11.30pm Mon-Sat, 6-11pm Sun; 🚌 all cross-city; 🚻 Ⓥ

People keep coming back to award-winning Monty's for its tasty dishes, which include *gorkhali* (chilli, yogurt and ginger chicken) or *kachela* (raw marinated meat), washed down with Shiva beer. Attentive staff mill around the shiny-dinky-trinket-filled room. It's convenient location opposite the Irish Film Institute (p78) makes it good for a post-movie bite.

🍴 QUEEN OF TARTS
Bakery-café €

☎ 670 7499; Cork Hill; ⏲ 7.30am-6pm Mon-Fri, from 9am Sat, from 10am Sun; 🚌 all cross-city; 🚻 Ⓥ

Queen of Tarts is the mother of all bakery-cafés, with its mouthwatering array of savoury tarts and filled focaccias, fruit crumbles, and sinful pastries. It's small, so get here early for lunch or get takeaway for the quiet garden at the Chester Beatty Library (p82) nearby.

🍴 TEA ROOMS
French/Modern Irish €€€€

☎ 407 0813; Clarence, 6-8 Wellington Quay; ⏲ 12.30-2.30pm Mon-Fri & Sun, 6.30-10.30pm Mon-Sat, to 9.30pm Sun; 🚌 all cross-city; 🚻 🚻 Ⓥ

Monty's of Kathmandu

The Tea Rooms' fortunes have been up and down in recent years, but things seem to have settled recently with the arrival of chef Fred Cordonnier. The Tea

Oliver St John Gogarty's

Rooms' rather ambitious menu features classic French cuisine – based equally on fish and meat – with an Irish twist. This is *haute cuisine* stripped of all pretension, leaving just solid, well-prepared seasonal food that is still beautifully presented and definitely a pleasure to eat.

🍸 DRINK
🍸 MULLIGANS

☎ 677 5582; 8 Poolbeg St; 🚌 14, 44, 47, 48, 62; 🚉 Tara Street; 🕓 to 5pm
Built in the 1850s, Mulligans seems to have changed little since then. A place for serious drinking, it is reputed to serve the best Guinness in Ireland and is popular with journalists from the nearby *Irish Times*. The pub appeared as the local in the film *My Left Foot* with Daniel Day-Lewis.

🍸 OCTAGON BAR

☎ 670 9000; Clarence, 6-8 Wellington Quay; 🚌 all cross-city; 🕓 good
This swish bar at the Clarence, owned by U2, has an odd atmosphere not helped by the artificial daylight and anodyne music policy. It's probably the only place in Temple Bar, though, where you'll find 30-something Dubliners or the odd resident celebrity having a quiet G&T.

☲ OLIVER ST JOHN GOGARTY'S

☎ 671 1822; 58-59 Fleet St; ◷ sessions 2.30-7pm & 9pm-2am Mon-Sat, noon-2pm, 5-7pm & 8.30pm-1am Sun; 🚌 all cross-city; ♿

The surprisingly authentic traditional music sessions at this jumping Temple Bar pub are extremely popular with tourists. Come early to get a seat.

☲ PALACE BAR

☎ 677 9290; 21 Fleet St; 🚌 all cross-city; ♿ to 6pm

With its mirrors, etched glass and wooden niches, Palace Bar is often said to be the perfect example of an old Dublin pub. It's popular with journalists from the nearby *Irish Times* and was patronised by writers Patrick Kavanagh and Flann O'Brien last century.

⭐ PLAY

☲ BOILERHOUSE SAUNA

☎ 677 3130; 12 Crane Lane; admission €20; ◷ 1pm-6am Sun-Thu, 24hr Fri & Sat; 🚌 all cross-city

This is a popular late-night destination for gay men looking to sweat it out after partying at George (p94), just around the corner. It's big and very clean and is reputed to be the best organised of Dublin's gay-oriented saunas.

MICRO-REVOLUTION

A number of microbreweries are challenging the supremacy of Guinness for the hearts and taste buds of Dubliners. One is **Messrs Maguire** (☎ 670 5777; 1-2 Burgh Quay), a gigantic 'überbar' spread across three levels that offers five of its own brews, from a creamy porter to the German-style Haus beer. Another is the **Dublin Brewing Company** (☎ 872 8622; www.dublinbrewing.com; 141-146 N King St; ◷ 9am-5.30pm Mon-Fri), which sells its four beers, including the well-loved brew Revolution Red, during business hours only.

The best known, however, is the **Porterhouse Brewing Company** (☎ 679 8847; www.porterhousebrewco.com; 16-18 Parliament St) in Temple Bar. Porterhouse is the brainchild of cousins Oliver Hughes and Liam Lahart who, in 1989, spotted a gap in the market for locally brewed beers. They soon learned not to underestimate Dubliner's thirst for a decent pint. From humble beginnings in their small Temple Bar brewery they expanded and now bring their 10 delicious lagers (including the award-winning Oyster stout) to appreciative swillers all across Ireland and the UK.

☲ HA'PENNY BRIDGE INN

☎ 677 0616; 42 Wellington Quay; admission €10/8; ◷ shows start 9pm Tue-Thu; 🚌 all cross-city

From Tuesday through Thursday you can hear some pretty funny

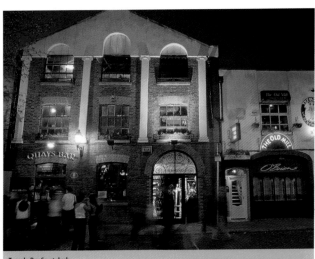

Temple Bar Sq at dusk

comedians (and some truly awful ones) do their shtick in the upstairs room of this Temple Bar institution that has remained unchanged since the '70s. Tuesday night's Battle of the Axe, an improv night that features a great deal of crowd participation, is the best.

☆ HUB
☎ 635 9991; 23 Eustace St; admission €6-15; ⏰ 8pm-late; 🚌 all cross-city
Arctic Monkeys, We Are Scientists and comedian Jimmy Carr have all graced the decks at the legendary rock-indie-electronic

night Trashed on Tuesdays, hosted by Trev Radiator. Otherwise Hub offers up a mixed bag of indie hits, and drinks promos for all and sundry.

☆ IRISH FILM INSTITUTE (IFI)
☎ 679 5744; www.irishfilm.ie; 6 Eustace St; matinees/evenings €7.50/8; ⏰ centre 10am-11.30pm; films 2-11pm; 🚌 all cross-city; ♿ good
The IFI shows classics and new independent flicks. You have to be a member to see a movie here, but you can buy a one-week membership with your ticket for

€1 per group. It has mother-and-baby screenings and the complex also has a bar, café and excellent bookshop.

⭐ MEZZ
☎ 670 7655; 23-24 Eustace St; admission free-€20; 🕐 to 2.30am Mon-Sat, to 11pm Sun; 🚌 all cross-city

Dark, sweaty and loud: it's the way music venues used to be in those heady days before standard lamps and leather sofas became, well, standard. Old-school rock, electronic, funk and garage bands belt it out most nights to a young up-for-it crowd.

⭐ OLYMPIA THEATRE
☎ 677 7744; 72 Dame St; 🕐 box office 10am-6.30pm Mon-Sat; 🚌 all cross-city; ♿

This is an ornate old Victorian music hall that specialises in light plays, comedy and, around Christmas time, panto. In recent years though, pleasantly tatty Olympia Theatre has gained more of a reputation for the live gigs it hosts, which have included performances by some big international acts.

⭐ PROJECT ARTS CENTRE
☎ 1850 260 027; www.project.ie; 39 E Essex St; 🕐 box office 11am-7pm Mon-Sat; 🚌 all cross-city; ♿ good; ♿

The Project Arts Centre's three stages (including a black box) are home to experimental plays from up-and-coming Irish and foreign writers. Some are brilliant, others execrable, but there's excitement in taking risks.

⭐ ROGUE
☎ 675 3971; 64 Dame St; admission €8-12; 🕐 11.30pm-3am Mon-Sat; 🚌 all cross-city

A relative newcomer on the block, Rogue is an intimate two-floored venue that is home to the Bodytonic crew who decamped from now-defunct Wax. Clubbers can expect to hear melodic and deep House and techno at the excellent Discotonic on Saturday nights.

⭐ TEMPLE BAR MUSIC CENTRE
TBMC; ☎ 670 9202; www.tbmc.ie; Curved St; 🕐 7.30pm-2.30am; 🚌 all cross-city

This place combines a live venue, club, bar and café with rehearsal rooms, music classes and recording studios. Though it's a bit sparse on comfort, plans are afoot for a major overhaul. In the meantime you'll find something on nightly to suit every taste, from funk and disco to guitar-driven indie rock.

>SODA

It's a made-up name (by us, thank you very much) but it refers to a very real and very distinctive neighbourhood – the stretch of streets that runs *So*uth of *Da*me St from Grafton St's western edge right to the eastern boundary of the Liberties. You'll find the city at its funkiest here, from the independently owned boutiques to the supercool bars and clubs that give the area its boho flavour. In fact, SoDa is making 'alternative' a personality. It's here you'll find Dublin's single best attraction in the Chester Beatty Library, plus groovy markets, alternative shops, atmospheric old pubs and the best ethnic eats in town. From superstylin' S William St to convivial Camden St, explore SoDa now before the developers take over.

SODA

◉ SEE
Chester Beatty Library ...	1	B2
Dublin Castle	2	B1
Shaw Birthplace	3	B6
Whitefriar Street		
Carmelite Church	4	B3

🛍 SHOP
A Store is Born	5	B2
Asia Food Market	6	C2
Ave Maria	7	C2
Barry Doyle		
Design Jewellers ...	8	C2
Blue Eriu	9	C1
Costume	10	C2
Decor	11	C4
George Street Arcade .	12	C2
Harlequin	(see 10)	
Inreda	13	C6
Jenny Vander	14	C2
Low Key	15	C2
Memorabilia	16	C2
Natural Shoe Store	17	C2
Neptune Gallery	18	C2
Tulle	19	C2
Vivien Walsh	20	C2
Walton's	21	C2
Wild Child	22	C2

🍴 EAT
Blazing Salads	23	C1
Brasil	24	B2
Café Bardeli	25	D2
Café Bardeli	26	C1
Chez Max	27	B1
Clarendon	28	C2
Cooke's	29	C2
Dakota	30	C2
Fallon & Byrne	31	C1
Govinda	32	B2
Honest to Goodness	33	C2
Jaipur	34	B2
Juice	35	B1
L'Gueuleton	36	C2
La Maison des		
Gourmets	(see 10)	
Lemon	37	C1
Leo Burdock's	38	A2
Liston's	39	C6
Odessa	40	C1
Simon's Place	41	C2
Sixty6	42	C2

🍸 DRINK
Anseo	43	C5
Bia Bar	44	C2
Carnival	45	C4
Dragon	46	C2
George	47	C1
Globe	(see 26)	
Grogan's Castle Lounge	48	C2
Jasmine	49	C2
Long Hall	50	B2
Market Bar	51	C2
Solas	52	B4
Stag's Head	53	C1

⭐ PLAY
Andrew's Lane Theatre	54	C1
Crawdaddy	55	C6
Devitt's	56	C5
JJ Smyth's	57	B2
Rí Rá	58	C1
Tripod	(see 55)	
Village	59	B4
Whelans	60	B5

Chester Beatty Library

SEE

CHESTER BEATTY LIBRARY

☎ 407 0750; www.cbl.ie; Dublin Castle, Great Ship St; admission free; ⏱ 10am-5pm Mon-Fri, 11am-5pm Sat, 1-5pm Sun, closed Mon Oct-Apr, free tours 1pm Wed, 3pm & 4pm Sun; 🚌 50, 51b, 77, 78a, 123; ♿ good; 👶 monthly kids workshops

The astounding collection of New York mining magnate Sir Alfred Chester Beatty (1875–1968) is the basis for one of Dublin's best, if less-visited, museums, winner of the prestigious Europe Museum of the Year in 2002. Inside you'll find manuscripts, books, bindings and calligraphies from around the world – including one of the best collections of Korans found anywhere in the West. See also p14.

DUBLIN CASTLE

☎ 677 7129; www.dublincastle.ie; Cork Hill, Dame St; admission €4.50/2-3.50; ⏱ 10am-4.45pm Mon-Fri, from 2pm Sat (State Apartments can be closed at short notice, call ahead to check); 🚌 50, 54, 56a, 77, 77a; ♿ limited

The stronghold of British power in Ireland for 700 years, Dublin Castle is mostly an 18th-century creation built on Norman and Viking foundations. Of the 13th-century Anglo-Norman fortress built on the site, only the record tower remains. Once the official residence of the British viceroys in

Ireland and now used by the Irish Government, a tour will appeal to history and architecture buffs. On Sunday and holidays free tours run every 30 minutes.

◉ SHAW BIRTHPLACE
☎ 475 0854; www.visitdublin.com; 33 Synge St; admission €6.70/5.70/19; ◷ 10am-1pm & 2-5pm Mon, Tue, Thu & Fri, 2-5pm Sat, Sun & hols May-Sep; 🚌 16, 19, 122

Entering through velvet drapes the atmospheric birthplace and museum on playwright George Bernard Shaw, an unassuming house on a sleepy terrace, is like stepping back in time to middle-class Victorian Dublin. The 'time machine' audio-tour (in several languages) has a wonderfully evocative soundscape full of witty asides about Victorian social mores.

◉ WHITEFRIAR STREET CARMELITE CHURCH
☎ 475 8821; 56 Aungier St; admission free; ◷ 8am-6.30pm, to 8.30pm Tue, to 7.30pm Sun; 🚌 16, 16a, 16c, 19, 19a, 65, 83; 🚻 good

On the former site of a Carmelite monastery, this huge church houses a 16th-century Flemish oak statue of the Mother and Child, thought to be the only one of its kind to survive the Reformation. The altar contains the remains of St Valentine, donated by Pope Gregory XVI in 1835.

JUSTICE FOR ALL?
The Figure of Justice that faces Dublin Castle's Upper Yard from the Cork Hill entrance has a controversial history. The statue was seen as a snub by many Dubliners, who felt Justice was symbolically turning her back on the city. If that wasn't enough, when it rained the scales would fill with water and tilt, rather than remaining perfectly balanced. Eventually a hole was drilled in the bottom of each pan, restoring balance, sort of.

🛍 SHOP

🛍 A STORE IS BORN
☎ 679 5866; 34 Clarendon St; ◷ 10am-6pm Sat; 🚌 all cross-city; 🚊 St Stephen's Green

Discretely hidden for six days a week behind a garage roller-door, this store opens up on Saturday to reveal a bounty of paisley dresses, peasant tops, belts, beads, cashmere cardies, sequined singlets, wide-collared men's shirts and suit pants.

🛍 ASIA FOOD MARKET
☎ 677 9764; 18 Drury St; ◷ 10am-7pm Mon-Sat; 🚌 16, 16a, 19, 19a, 65, 83; 🚊 St Stephen's Green

This large, friendly food emporium should be your first port of call if you want to whip up an Asian-feast. For a start it's really good value and you'll find everything here from kitchen implements to hard-to-come-by ingredients such as grass jelly, habanero chillies, brown basmati rice or – should you wish – chicken's feet.

☐ AVE MARIA
☎ 671 8229; 38 Clarendon St; ⊙ 10am-6pm Mon-Wed, Fri & Sat, to 7pm Thu; 🚍 all cross-city; 🚇 St Stephen's Green
If Tina Turner were in Dublin, she'd shop here. Glam up with neon net, sequinned and satin cocktail dresses from Queenie, Manoush and Consumer Guide and some seriously bling costume jewels.

☐ BARRY DOYLE DESIGN JEWELLERS
☎ 671 2838; George's St Arcade; ⊙ 9am-6pm Mon-Wed, Fri & Sat, to 8pm Thu; 🚍 15, 16, 19, 83
Upstairs on the southern side of George's St Arcade, Barry Doyle works away in his light-filled, wooden studio producing beautiful, bold, handmade necklaces, bracelets and rings in Celtic and modern designs. Individual pieces can be commissioned – prices are steep but the work is of excellent quality.

☐ BLUE ERIU
☎ 672 5776; 7 S William St; ⊙ 10am-8pm Mon-Thu, to 6pm Fri & Sat; 🚍 all cross-city
In a fantastic, otherworldly space, Blue Eriu sells top-end skincare, cosmetics and haircare from Prada,

PASSION FOR FASHION
After years in the wilderness, Irish designers are making a name for themselves on the international fashion stage. John Rocha, whose own-label clothes have been high fashion for the past decade, has branched into homewares (available in Brown Thomas, p42) and hotel design, as has milliner to the supermodels Philip Treacy, who recently designed the flamboyant G Hotel in Galway. Irish names currently making a splash internationally include Joanne Hynes, Pauric Sweeney and N & C Kilkenny.

Shu Uemura and Kleins, as well as scented candles, oils and artisan perfumes. Facials and massages are pricey but highly regarded.

☐ COSTUME
☎ 679 4188; 10 Castle Market; ⊙ 10am-6pm Mon-Wed, Fri & Sat, to 7pm Thu; 🚍 all cross-city; 🚇 St Stephen's Green
From casuals to sparkly full-length dresses, Costume specialises in stylish contemporary women's wear from young European designers. Its own Costume label sits alongside pieces by Temperley, Anna Sui, newcomer Jonathan Saunders and Irish label Leighlee (see p72).

☐ DECOR
☎ 475 9010; 14a Wexford St; ⊙ 10am-6pm Mon-Sat; 🚍 16, 16a, 16c, 19, 19a, 65, 83; 🚇 St Stephen's Green

George's St Arcade

Decor is crammed with chunky teak and mahogany furniture from Southeast Asia, basalt Buddha statues, off-beat gilded mirrors and exotic throws – and all at a price we like, to boot.

🖼 GEORGE'S STREET ARCADE

🕙 10am-6pm Mon-Sat; 🚌 all cross-city

Dublin's best nonfood market (there's sadly not much competition) is sheltered within an elegant Victorian Gothic arcade between S Great George's and Drury Sts. Apart from shops and stalls selling new and old clothes, second-hand books, hats, posters, jewellery and records, there's a fortune teller, gourmet nibbles and a fish and chipper who does a roaring trade.

🖼 HARLEQUIN

☎ 671 0202; 13 Castle Market; 🕙 10.30am-6pm Mon-Wed, Fri & Sat, to 7pm Thu; 🚌 all cross-city; 🚉 St Stephen's Green

A fantastically cluttered shop, jam-packed with authentic vintage clothing from the 1920s onwards, as well as satin gloves, top hats, snakeskin bags and jet-beaded chokers.

🖻 INREDA
☎ 478 0362; 71 Lower Camden St;
🕑 10.30am-6pm Mon-Fri, 11am-6pm
Sat; 🚍 16, 16a, 19, 19a, 65, 83
Inreda is a virtual shrine for Scandi-navian design enthusiasts to revere beautifully-crafted modern furni-ture by Swedese and David Design, as well as lighting, ceramics, glassware and accessories by Design House Stockholm. It's pricey stuff but there's no harm in looking, right?

🖻 JENNY VANDER
☎ 677 0406; 50 Drury St; 🕑 10am-5.45pm Mon-Sat; 🚍 all cross-city; 🚈 St
Stephen's Green
More *Breakfast at Tiffany's* than *Hair*, this second-hand store ooz-es elegance and sophistication. Exquisite beaded handbags, fur-trimmed coats, richly patterned dresses and costume jewellery priced as if it were the real thing are snapped up by discerning fashionistas and film stylists.

🖻 LOW KEY
☎ 677 0299; 23 Georges St Arcade;
🕑 9.30am-6pm Mon-Wed, Fri & Sat, to
8pm Thu, 2-6pm Sun; 🚍 15, 16, 19, 83
Low-key boutique stocked with oversized jeans and sweatshirts, surfy dresses and low-slung jeans for boys and girls who prefer understated cool to glitzy glam.

Labels include Fever, St Martin, Snob and Dollar.

🖻 MEMORABILIA
☎ 679 4699; 47 Drury St; 🕑 9.30am-5.30pm Mon-Wed, Fri & Sat, to 7pm Thu;
🚍 all cross-city
What do you buy someone who seems to have everything? More stuff, of course. This new shop for solvent Celtic tiger pups trades in original (mostly sports) memora-bilia from Buzz Aldrin's moon-walker medal to autographed movie posters.

🖻 NATURAL SHOE STORE
☎ 671 4978; 25 Drury St; 🕑 9am-5.30pm Mon-Sat; 🚍 all cross-city;
🚈 St Stephen's Green
Give your feet a treat at this tiny, spartan shop that specialises in natural, comfortable shoes. Apart from therapeutic but cool Birkenstocks and Komodos, there are 'vegetarian' shoes and shoes handmade by a shoemaker in Cork.

🖻 NEPTUNE GALLERY
☎ 671 5021; 1st fl, 41 S William St;
🕑 10am-5.30pm Mon-Fri, 10am-1pm
Sat; 🚍 all cross-city
Climb the rickety stairs over Busyfeet Café into this Aladdin's Cave of cartography. Pick up dusty maps and prints of Ireland dating

from 1600 to 1880 for anything from a few quid up to €1000.

▢ TULLE

☎ 679 9115; 28 George's St Arcade; ⏱ 10am-6pm Mon-Wed, Fri & Sat, to 8pm Thu; 🚌 all cross-city; 🚆 St Stephen's Green

Australian designers Sass & Bide and Wheels & Doll Baby, plus Euro designers Fornarina and Sonia Rykiel, are stocked in this outlet for fashion-savvied young gals.

▢ VIVIEN WALSH

☎ 475 5031; 24 Lower Stephen St; ⏱ 11am-6pm Mon-Wed & Fri, to 7pm Thu, 10am-6pm Sat; 🚌 15, 16, 19, 83; 🚆 St Stephen's Green

One of Ireland's best-known jewellery designers, Vivien Walsh uses Swarovski crystal, glass, feathers, pearls and beads to create delicate, fantastical pieces that hark back to the 1920s. The elaborate necklaces, in vivid turquoise, pink, purple and green, are quite an investment, but simple bracelets can be had for under €40. French and Italian leather bags and shoes complement the displays.

▢ WALTON'S

☎ 475 0661; 69-70 S Great George's St; ⏱ 9am-6pm Mon-Sat, noon-5pm Sun; 🚌 16, 16a, 19, 19a, 65, 83

These traditional music specialists sell CDs, instruments, sheet music for Irish harp, flute and fiddle, and song books featuring tunes by Irish music greats, including the Wolfe Tones, the Fureys and the Dubliners. You can also take two-hour crash courses in the *bodhrán* (Irish drums) or tin whistle at its music school. God bless the staff.

▢ WILD CHILD

☎ 475 5099; 61 S Great George's St; ⏱ 10am-6pm Mon-Wed, Fri & Sat, to 7pm Thu, 1-6pm Sun; 🚌 16, 16a, 16c, 19, 19a, 65, 83; 🚆 St Stephen's Green

If you're in the market for a groovy batik wall hangings, Eames chairs or funky Melamine kitchen containers you've come to the right place. Preview new stock among the hand-picked retro furniture from the 1950s onwards, on the first Sunday of the month.

🍴 EAT

🍴 BRASIL *Brazilian*   €€

☎ 405 3854; 17 Upper Stephen's St; ⏱ noon-11pm, to 4pm Mon; 🚌 all cross-city; ♿

Transport yourself to the heady streets of Rio at this charming little *churrascaria* (barbecue). The place feels authentic right down to the Brazilian staff, salsa music and plastic tablecloths. A buffet-style blow-out of grilled meats, black beans, rice and cassava, washed down with *capirinhas* (rum cocktails) will have you dancing lambada like a native.

🍴 BRETZEL BAKERY *Bakery* €
☎ 475 2724; 1a Lennox St; ⏰ 8.30am-3pm Mon, to 6pm Tue, Wed & Fri, to 7pm Thu, 9am-5pm Sat, 9am-1pm Sun; 🚌 14, 15, 65, 83

The bagels might be a bit on the chewy side, but they've got their charms – as do the scrumptious selections of breads, savoury snacks, cakes and biscuits that have locals queuing out the door on weekends. Certified kosher since 2003, Bretzel Bakery has been on this Portobello site since 1870.

🍴 CAFÉ BARDELI *Italian* €€
☎ 677 1646; 12-13 S Great George's St; ⏰ 12.30-11pm, 2-10pm Sun; 🚌 15, 16, 19, 83; ♿ 👶 V

Two new branches, **Grafton St branch** (Map p39, B4; ☎ 672 7720; Grafton St; ⏰ noon-11pm Thu-Sat, to 10pm Sun-Wed; 🚇 Stephen's Green) and **Ranelagh St branch** (☎ 496 1886; 62 Ranelagh St; ⏰ 12.30-11pm, to 10pm Sun; 🚌 11, 18, 44, 48), testify to the success of this eternally popular restaurant's simple formula: great crispy pizzas with imaginative toppings such as spicy lamb and tzatziki, fresh homemade pastas or salads such as broccoli, feta and chickpea that you'll dream about for days. All at prices that won't break the bank in a buzzing atmosphere. What more could you want, hey?

VEGETARIAN OPTIONS
Dublin has a surprising number of good vegetarian restaurants as well as a considerable number of regular restaurants offering a reasonable selection of things to graze on. The following vegetarian restaurants also have vegan dishes:
> Blazing Salads (☎ 671 9552; 42 Drury St; ⏰ 9am-5.30pm Mon-Sat)
   Excellent salad bar and sandwiches, but no seating.
> Café Fresh (Map p39, A3; ☎ 671 9669; Powerscourt Centre; ⏰ 9am-5pm Mon-Sat)
   Hot meals, smoothies, juices, soups and great salads.
> Cornucopia (Map p39, A3; ☎ 677 7583; 19 Wicklow St; ⏰ 8.30am-8pm Mon-Wed, Fri & Sat, to 9pm Thu, noon-7pm Sun) Old-school country-kitchen-style restaurant with hearty hot dishes and brekkies.
> Govinda (☎ 475 0309; 4 Aungier St; ⏰ noon-9pm Mon-Sat) Run by Hare Krishnas, with Eastern hot meals and salads.
> Juice (☎ 475 7856; 73-83 S Great George's St; ⏰ 11am-11pm Mon-Sat, to 5pm Sun) Hip Pacific rim fare and organic wines.

🍴 CHEZ MAX *French* €€

☎ 633 7215; 1 Palace St; ⏲ 8am-10pm Mon-Thu, to 10.30pm Fri, 11am-11pm Sat & Sun; 🚌 16, 19, 83; ♿

Sitting at a little check-cloth table with a cheeky burgundy, listening to Edith Piaf you could easily daydream yourself back to 1940s Provence. Max's menu, from his home turf in Lozère – frog's legs, garlicky snails, *crôque monsieur* (toasted ham and cheese sand-wich), salmon with sorrel – has been around for nearly a century. *Plus ça change.*

🍴 CLARENDON
Modern European €€

☎ 679 2909; 32 Clarendon St; ⏲ noon-3pm & 5-9.30pm Mon-Thu, noon-6pm Fri-Sun; 🚌 15, 16, 19, 83; 🚇 Stephen's Green; ♿ 🚻 Ⓥ

Run by those canny boys from Bang Cafe (p62), this is bar food *par excellence*. Fish cakes, delicious salad, linguine with meatballs or sirloin steak with oyster mushrooms – come sample 'em all. And if you sit outdoors, you'll catch a tender tune or two wafting over from the open windows of the Conservatory of Music across the street.

🍴 COOKE'S
Modern European €€€

☎ 679 0536; 14 S William St; ⏲ noon-4.30pm Mon-Sat, 6-11pm Tue-Sat; 🚌 all cross-city; Ⓥ

Chez Max

Having undergone many incarna-tions, adventurous chef Johnny Cooke makes a welcome return to the kitchen with his latest venture. His loyal well-heeled lady and business clientele clamour for duck *confit* with Tuscan white bean, sublime beef carpaccio or – if they're feeling reckless – the surprise menu (€60 per person).

🍴 DAKOTA
Modern European €€

☎ 672 7696; 8-9 S William St; ⏲ noon-9pm Mon-Fri, to 8pm Sat, to 6pm Sun; 🚌 all cross-city; 🚻 Ⓥ

On a fine day grab an outdoor table and watch life go by with this menu that raises the bar (ahem) on pub grub; ribs with molasses and boubon sauce, beetroot houmous, lime tempura fish and mezze plates to share packed with baked haloumi, mango and other delectables.

🍴 FALLON & BYRNE
Foodhall €€€

☎ 472 1000; Exchequer St; ⏰ 9.30am-7pm Mon-Sat, noon-6pm Sun; 🚌 18, 83; ♿ fair; 🚶 V

The much anticipated opening of an upmarket foodhall, wine cellar and restaurant in the style of New York's Dean & Deluca caused a great stir among Dublin's food cognoscenti mid-2006. The chic buzzy brasserie with long red banquettes, diverse menu of creamy fish pie, beef carpaccio or roast turbot and excellent service hasn't failed to impress either.

🍴 HONEST TO GOODNESS
Café €

☎ 677 5373; George's St Arcade; ⏰ 9am-6pm Mon-Sat, noon-4pm Sun; 🚌 15, 16, 19, 83; 🚶 V

Wholesome sandwiches – such as beef, caramelised onion and horse-radish – imaginative breakfasts, homemade soups and smoothies are found in this funky little caff. Add delicious home-baked goodies and fair-trade coffee, all at rock bottom prices? Niiice.

🍴 JAIPUR *Indian* €€

☎ 677 0999; 43-46 S Great George's St; ⏰ 5-11pm; 🚌 15, 16, 19, 83; ♿ 🚶 V

The words 'minimalist' and 'Indian restaurant' aren't common design bedfellows in these parts, but

Fallon & Byrne

Jaipur is the exception. With massive glass windows and ne'er a patterned wallpaper in sight, this buzzing place serves up delicious Indian specialities such as Kashmiri lamb, *roghan josh* (rich, spicy lamb curry) and Goan seafood curry.

¶ L'GUELETON *French* €€

☎ 675 3708; 1 Fade St; ⏲ 12.30-3pm & 6-10pm Mon-Sat; 🚌 18, 83; ♿

The name's a bit of a mouthful (it means 'a meal with friends' we're told), and it doesn't have a sign or take bookings, but rising-star chef Troy McGuire and his team do the country French food thing damn well. If you can bag a table, feast on fennel-fragranced Carlingford oysters, snail and roquefort pithivier or lip-smacking *steak-frites* at prices you'll also enjoy.

¶ LA MAISON DES GOURMETS
French café €€

☎ 672 7258; 15 Castle Market; ⏲ 9am-6pm Mon-Sat; 🚌 15, 16, 19, 83

The city's Francophiles amass at this tiny French café above a bakery – and for good reason. The menu is small but its *tartines* (open sandwiches), with daily toppings such as roast aubergine and pesto, salad specials or plates of charcuterie are divine. Dream of Provence with a traditional country breakfast of meats, cheeses and warm crusty bread. You can

also make your own Gallic feast from the downstairs deli's selection of cheeses, brioches, cakes, bread and handmade chocolates.

¶ LEMON *Creperie* €

☎ 672 9044; 66 S William St; ⏲ 8am-7.30pm Mon-Wed & Fri, to 9pm Thu, 9am-7.30pm Sat, 10am-6.30pm Sun; 🚌 all cross-city; ♿ V

Lemon, which has a second **branch** (☎ 672 8898; 61 Dawson St), doesn't look like much – until you catch a whiff of those crepes. Then it's straight inside where a sweet or savoury crepe or waffle is yours in breakneck speed. Get it smothered in sinful ice cream, chocolate sauce, coconut or Grand Marnier.

¶ LEO BURDOCK'S
Takeaway café €

☎ 454 0306; 2 Werburgh St; ⏲ noon-midnight; 🚌 all cross-city

A long queue snakes down the road at any hour of the day outside this Dublin institution. And there's a reason for it: thick-cut, real potato chips and crispy fish wrapped in newspaper to go. Sometimes you just have to do it.

¶ LISTON'S *Deli* €

☎ 405 4779; 25 Camden St; ⏲ 8.30am-7.30pm Mon-Thu, to 6.30pm Fri, 10am-6pm Sat; 🚌 14, 14a, 15, 83; ♿ V

Karen Liston knows a thing or two about food, as the lunchtime queues out the door testify. Her combination of rustic breads filled with fresh, delicious fillings, incredible salads, salmon potato cakes and chocolate squares will have you lining up again and again.

🍴 ODESSA *Mediterranean* €€€
☎ 670 7634; 13-14 Dame Ct; ⏲ 6-11pm, 11.30am-4.30pm Sat & Sun; 🚌 all cross-city; 👶 V

Join the city's hipsters for home-made burgers, steaks or daily fish specials in Odessa's loungy atmosphere, complete with comfy sofas and retro lamps. Now with private member's club upstairs, you can celeb-watch through the window and weep. Weekend brunch is extremely popular: you were warned.

🍴 SIMON'S PLACE *Café* €
☎ 679 7821; George's St Arcade; ⏲ 8.30am-6pm Mon-Sat; 🚌 all cross-city; 👶 V

Simon hasn't had to change the menu of doorstep sandwiches and wholesome vegetarian soups since he first opened shop two decades ago, and why should he? His grub is as heartening and leg-endary as he is. It's a great place to mull over a coffee and watch life go by in the old-fashioned arcade.

🍴 SIXTY6 *American* €€
☎ 400 5878; 66-67 S Great George's St; ⏲ 8am-10.15pm Mon-Thu, 10am-11pm Fri & Sat, to 10.30pm Sun; 🚌 16, 19, 83; 👶 fair; 👶 high-chairs; V

This long, loud dining room has been doing a roaring trade since it opened in 2005. Looks like young Dubliners can't get enough of its buzzing atmosphere and Ameri-can-style menu of meatloaf, char-grilled mahi mahi, roast chicken on a spit or crayfish salad.

🍸 DRINK

🍸 ANSEO
18 Lower Camden St; 🚌 16, 83, 123

This place might not look much on the outside, or the inside for that matter – with its bog-standard carpet and chrome décor – but those underground scenesters Monkey Tennis work their magic on Friday nights, rocking the house with everything from Hot Chip to Velvet Underground.

🍸 BIA BAR
☎ 405 3563; 30 Lower Stephen St; 🚌 83, 123; 👶 to 7pm

A new bar with old-school smarts. These folks know how to keep a punter coming back: fast and friendly staff, DJs, a young eye-candy crowd and most important-ly, one of the centre's biggest beer gardens, complete with pebbled floor and palm trees.

Billy Scurry,
Chef at Gruel, DJ

My favourite restaurant is L'Gueuleton (p91). It has the nicest room of any in the city and the menu is of a very high standard – even if it doesn't change often enough. And the prices are excellent, considering the quality of the cuisine. I also love the no-reservations policy: it's egalitarian and treats everyone exactly the same, irrespective of who you are or who you know.

For live music, my choice would be Vicar Street (p107) – the wide stage means that no matter where you're seated you're never that far from the action, and it helps that generally the acts are usually top class. If I want to hear some good DJs, I'm usually spoilt for choice: the Globe (p94) and the bars along Wexford and Camden Sts – Carnival (p94), Solas (p95) and Anseo (p92) – are always good; for clubbing, I like Tripod (p96), which has always managed to reinvent itself and get a nice vibe going.

☏ CARNIVAL

☎ 405 3604; 11 Wexford St; ⏲ 2pm-midnight Sun-Thu, to 1am Fri & Sat; 🚌 83, 123; ♿ to 7pm

A party atmosphere and candle-lit, down-at-heel room makes Dermot Doran's latest venture a great place to meet people. Don't expect to chat though – the music from those DJs, playing everything from Magic Numbers to Kraftwerk (Thursday to Sunday), will drown out those witticisms.

☏ DRAGON

☎ 478 1590; 64-65 S Great George's St; ⏲ 5-11.30pm, to 2.30am Thu-Sat, to 11pm Sun; 🚌 all cross-city

The latest addition to Dublin's gay scene, this disco bar with colourful Asian décor, comfy booths and small dance floor attracts young pre-George (below) revellers.

☏ GEORGE

☎ 478 2983; 89 S Great George's St; admission most nights after 10pm €5-8; ⏲ 12.30-11.30pm Mon & Tue, to 3am Wed-Sat, to 1am Sun; 🚌 all cross-city

You can't miss the bright-purple George, Dublin's best-known gay bar, which has a reputation for becoming ever more wild and wacky as the night progresses. At 6.30pm on Sunday it is packed for an enormously popular bingo night, while Thursday night is the Missing Link game show hosted by Annie Balls.

☏ GLOBE

☎ 671 1220; 11 S Great George's St; 🚌 all cross-city; ♿ to 7pm

Dublin's original and best café-bar is a mecca for hip young locals and clued-in visitors. With its wooden floors and brick walls, it's as much a daytime haunt for a good latte as a watering hole by night. Eclectic music, Sunday-afternoon jazz and friendly staff help the place thrive. It has recently changed hands but the new owners will hardly try to fix what ain't broke.

☏ GROGAN'S CASTLE LOUNGE

☎ 677 9320; 15 S William St; 🚌 all cross-city; ♿ to 7pm

Known simply as Grogan's (after the original owner), this old place is a city-centre institution. Long patronised by writers, painters and other bohemian types (whose work it often displays in the walls), it's laid-back and contemplative much of the day. Oddly, drinks are slightly cheaper in the stone-floor bar than in the carpeted lounge.

☏ JASMINE

☎ 670 4000; Brook's Hotel, Drury St; ⏲ 10am-11pm Mon-Thu, 11.30am-12.30am Fri & Sat, to 11pm Sun; ♿ good; ♿

Know your Bushmills from your Ballantine's, or Chivas from Canadian Club? Pull a pew up to the sleek bar, where head barman Michael

Foggarty has amassed more than 80 whiskeys and earned himself a place on *Whiskey* magazine's list of great whiskey bars of the world. Damn fine cocktails too.

☒ LONG HALL
☎ 475 1590; 51 S Great George's St; 🚌 16, 16a, 19, 19a, 65, 83; 🕓 to 6pm
With wildly ornate Victorian woodwork, mirrors and chandeliers, this is one of the city's most beautiful and best-loved pubs. From musk-coloured walls to mirrored columns behind the bar, it's all elegantly dingy. The bartenders are experts at their craft, an increasingly rare sight in Dublin these days.

☒ MARKET BAR
☎ 613 9094; 14a Fade St; 🚌 all cross-city; 🚻 good; 🕓
High ceilings, bench seating and the din of a chatty crowd give this huge former sausage factory the atmosphere of Grand Central Station on Christmas Eve. It's fashionable, friendly, the tapas are great and staff even bring drinks to your table. Check out the wonderful bar made from dipped-brass bank doors.

☒ SOLAS
☎ 478 0583; 31 Wexford St; 🕓 9.30am-12.30am Sun-Wed, to 1.30am Thu-Sat; 🚌 83, 121; 🚻 fair; 🕓
Wexford and Camden Sts are fast becoming the golden mile of the

indie scene, with dark and loungy Solas current kingpin. Late opening, nightly DJs, a funky rooftop beer garden and its proximity to Whelans and the Village all add to its vibe. Oh, and of course the loos that flush rain water.

☒ STAG'S HEAD
☎ 679 3701; 1 Dame Ct; 🚌 all cross-city; 🕓 to 6pm
Built in 1770 but remodelled in 1895 at the height of Victorian opulence, this pub has magnificent stained glass, chandeliers and marble, carved wood and, of

Stag's Head

course, mounted stags' heads. It can get crowded but it's worth it; the food's pretty good too.

⭐ PLAY

⭐ ANDREW'S LANE THEATRE
☎ 679 5720; www.andrewslane.com; 9-17 St Andrew's Lane; admission free-€18; ⏰ box office 10.30am-7pm Mon-Sat; 🚌 all cross-city; ♿ good; 🚼
A well-established, commercial-fringe theatre that shows work by touring local companies and overseas productions, often comedy or light drama.

⭐ CRAWDADDY
☎ 478 0166; Harcourt St; ⏰ 7.30pm-3am Wed-Sat; 🚌 14, 15, 48a; 🚇 Harcourt
Part of the old Harcourt Street station complex, this stylish speakeasy attracts international jazz, folk and soul acts who enjoy the intimacy here. There are also rising local stars cutting their teeth in front of a largely appreciative audience.

⭐ DEVITT'S
☎ 475 3414; 78 Lower Camden St; admission free; ⏰ from 9.30pm Thu-Sat
As good as any traditional music session you'll hear in the city centre, Devitt's – aka the Hogan Stand – is one of the favourite place for the city's talented musicians to display their wares. Highly recommended.

⭐ JJ SMYTH'S
☎ 475 2565; 12 Aungier St; admission €8-10; ⏰ most shows start 8.30-9.30pm; 🚌 16, 16a, 19, 19a, 65, 83
Jazz and blues at this small but legendary pub draw a regular crowd. The Irish Blues Club plays on Tuesday and long-standing resident bands as well as international guest acts play every other night except Wednesday.

⭐ RÍ RÁ
☎ 677 4835; Dame Ct; admission €8-12; ⏰ 11.30pm-3am Mon-Sat; 🚌 all cross-city
One of the city's friendlier clubs, this place is for people who like their music without frenetic beats. Refreshingly, the bouncers here are friendly, funny and very fair. The emphasis is mostly on funk, old and new, though Monday's '80s-fest Strictly Handbag is now in its 16th year. Upstairs the Globe bar converts into a chilled-out drink and chat area.

⭐ TRIPOD
☎ 478 0166; www.pod.ie; 35 Harcourt St; ⏰ 11pm-3am Thu-Sat; 🚌 14, 15, 65, 83; 🚇 Harcourt
Launched in late 2006 in the atmospheric old Harcourt Street station, Tripod integrates three venues (geddit?): a state-of-the-art 1300-capacity live rock and pop music venue, a smaller dance

club and the intimate live venue Crawdaddy (opposite).

⭐ VILLAGE

☎ 475 8555; 30 Wexford St; ⏰ noon-2.30am Mon-Sat, noon-1am Sun; 🚌 16, 16a, 19, 19a, 65, 83

This large venue is surprisingly cosy for its size. All wooden cladding and warm lighting, the downstairs free bar packs 'em in for its late licence. Upstairs, the venue puts on medium-sized international and home-grown rock and pop acts most nights.

⭐ WHELANS

☎ 478 0766; www.whelanslive.com; 26 Wexford St (enter via Camden Row); admission €10-25; ⏰ doors open 8pm; 🚌 14, 15, 65, 83

A good gig here can be quite magical. The crowd gathers round the elevated central stage and more peer down from the circular balcony – everyone mouthing the words to their favourite songs and ballads. Whelans has an interesting parade of fine local and international singer-songwriters – well worth a look.

Tripod

>KILMAINHAM & THE LIBERTIES

Light on entertainment but laden with sights – including the city's most visited attraction (the temple of Guinness) – Kilmainham and the Liberties are among the oldest neighbourhoods in Dublin. The historical wealth and cultural significance of these areas draw tourists from far and near, which has translated into a roaring trade in art and antiques.

Dublin's most staunchly traditional neighbourhood, the Liberties, is due for a facelift. A much-trumpeted development, the Digital Hub – intended to radically modernise the area – has fallen flat, but urban rejuvenation is inevitable. It's just a matter of when…

KILMAINHAM & THE LIBERTIES

📷 SEE
Bad Art Gallery 1 H3
Christ Church Cathedral 2 H2
Cross Gallery 3 H3
Dvblinia 4 H2
Guinness Storehouse 5 F3
Irish Museum
of Modern Art 6 D3
James Joyce
House of the Dead 7 G2
Kilmainham Gaol 8 C3

Marsh's Library 9 H3
Mother's Tankship 10 F2
St Audoen's
Protestant Church 11 H2
St Patrick's Cathedral .. 12 H3
Sharkey Gallery 13 H3

🛍 SHOP
Design Associates 14 G3
Fleury Antiques 15 H3
Niall Mullen's 16 G2

O'Sullivan Antiques..... 17 H3
Oxfam Home 18 H3

🍸 DRINK
Brazen Head **19** G2

⭐ PLAY
Vicar Street 20 G2

Please see over for map

◉ SEE

◉ BAD ART GALLERY

☎ 087 991 0650; www.thebadart gallerydublin.com; 79 Francis St; admission free; ⏱ 10.30am-6pm Mon-Sat; 🚌 51b, 78a, 121, 123; ♿ good
This new tongue-in-cheek gallery for emerging students and contemporary Irish artists specialises in big, bold and affordable art. Deborah Donnelly paints brash, colourful portraits of cows, cakes and circus tents. Get there for opening nights when the room is flamboyantly dressed.

◉ CHRIST CHURCH CATHEDRAL

☎ 677 8099; www.cccdub.ie; Christ Church Pl; admission €5/2.50/7; ⏱ 9am-6pm Mon-Fri Jun-Aug, 9.45am-5pm or 6pm Mon-Fri Sep-May, 10am-4.30pm Sat, 12.45-2.45pm Sun, choral evensong 5pm Thu & Sat, 3.30pm Sun, bell-ringing 7-9pm Fri (practice), 10-11am & 2.30-3.30pm Sun & New Year's Eve; 🚌 50, 66, 77, 121, 123
Dublin's most imposing church and famed landmark, Christ Church Cathedral lies within the city's original Norse settlement and the old heart of medieval Dublin. It was commissioned in 1172 by the Anglo-Norman conqueror of Dublin, Richard de Clare, 'Strongbow', whose tomb is just inside the main door, and Archbishop Laurence O'Toole.

THE BELLS, THE BELLS
The melodic sound of Christ Church's bells has been ringing through Dublin air since 1670. Nineteen bells, the greatest number rung in this way worldwide and weighing up to 2.25 tonnes each, are hand rung in a mathematical sequence, with training taking years to complete.

Try to visit just before choral evensong to catch the choir's wonderfully evocative recitals, which bring the cathedral's rich atmosphere to life.

◉ CROSS GALLERY

☎ 473 8978; www.crossgallery.ie; 59 Francis St; admission free; ⏱ 10am-5.30pm Tue-Fri, 11am-4pm Sat; 🚌 51b, 78a, 121, 123; ♿ good
Nestled among the top-end antique stores of the Liberties, Cross is an open-plan gallery in a terraced house designed to be unintimidating (in both design and price) to first time buyers. Contemporary and abstract artists such as Clea Van der Grijn, Simon English and Laurent Mellet are represented.

◉ DVBLINIA

☎ 679 4611; Christ Church; admission €6/5/16, under 5yr free; ⏱ 10am-5pm Apr-Sep, 11am-4pm Mon-Sat, 10am-4.30pm Sun Oct-Mar; 🚌 51b, 78a, 123; ♿ good
Inside what was once Christ Church's Synod Hall, Dvblinia

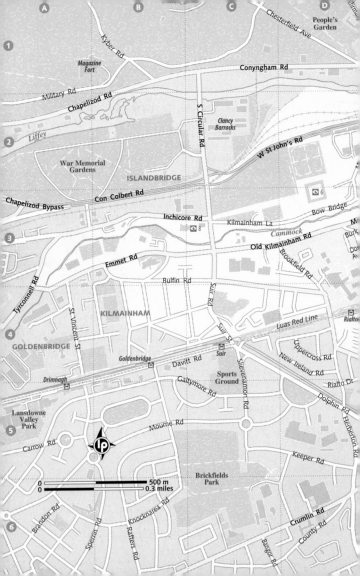

Irish Museum of Modern Art (IMMA)

re-creates medieval Dublin using models, music, streetscapes and interactive displays. Adults might find it a bit kitsch, but kids will love the hands-on archaeology room and re-created medieval fair – with simple but fun activities at each stall. Make your own brass rubbing, try on armour or try to knock medieval man's nose with a ball. You can climb St Michael's Tower for panoramic views of the city.

◉ GUINNESS STOREHOUSE
☎ 408 4800; www.guinness-store house.com; St James's Gate; admission €14/9.50, under 6 yr free, discounts apply for online bookings; ⏲ 9.30am-9pm Jul & Aug, 9.30am-5pm Sep-Jun; 🚌 51b, 78a, 123; 🚃 St James'; ♿ excellent

Like Disneyland for beer lovers, the Guinness Storehouse is an all-singing, all-dancing extravaganza combining sophisticated exhibits with more than a pintful of marketing. The highlight of a visit to the museum – housed in an old grain store opposite the original St James's Gate Brewery – is a glass of Guinness in the Gravity Bar at the top of the building. See also p12.

◉ IRISH MUSEUM OF MODERN ART (IMMA)
☎ 612 9900; www.modernart.ie; Military Rd, Kilmainham; admission free; ⏲ 10am-5.30pm Tue-Sat, from noon Sun & hols, exhibition tours 2.30pm Wed, Fri & Sun; 🚌 26, 51, 78a, 79, 90, 123; ♿ good

Ireland's premier gallery of contemporary art is at the Royal Hospital, Kilmainham, a striking 17th-century building whose design is inspired by Les Invalides in Paris and which served the same purpose, as a hospice for retired soldiers. Even if contemporary art doesn't float your boat, a wander around this extraordinary building is a must. See also p15.

◐ JAMES JOYCE HOUSE OF THE DEAD

☎ 086 157 9546; 15 Usher's Quay; admission €10/5-8, under 6 yr free; ☉ 10am-5pm; 🚌 25x, 26, 46a, 78, 79, 90, 92; 🚹 none

The restoration of the setting for James Joyce's story *The Dead* has been a labour of love for barrister Brendan Kilty. As a museum there aren't many actual artefacts (besides touring exhibitions) but walking through the crumbling rooms that are almost as they were when Joyce spent Christmases there with his aunts is very special.

◑ KILMAINHAM GAOL

☎ 453 5984; www.heritageireland .ie; Inchicore Rd; admission by 90min tour only, €5.30/2.10-3.70/11.50; ☉ 9.30am-6pm Apr-Sep, to 5.30pm Mon-Fri, 10am-6pm Sun Oct-Mar, last admission 90min before closing; 🚹 limited, call ahead

One of Dublin's most sobering sights, Kilmainham Gaol oozes centuries of pain, oppression and suffering from its decrepit limestone hulk. Scene of countless emotional episodes along Ireland's rocky road to independence, the jail was home to many of the country's political heroes, martyrs and villains. Enjoy the visit! For more, see p18.

◐ MARSH'S LIBRARY

☎ 454 3511; www.marshlibrary.ie; St Patrick's Cl; admission €2.50/1.25; ☉ 10am-1pm & 2-5pm Mon & Wed-Fri, 10.30am-1pm Sat; 🚌 50, 50a, 54, 54a, 56a

Virtually unchanged for 300 years, Marsh's Library is a glorious example of an 18th-century scholar's den. In fact, it is one of the few buildings from that time

A SCHOLASTIC SOLOMON

Englishman Narcissus Marsh (1638–1713), an Oxford graduate and Archbishop of Armagh and Dublin and six times Lord Justice of Ireland, must have been a formidable chap. As provost of Trinity college he was an ardent supporter of the Irish language and, believing that knowledge is king, was shocked to find there was nowhere in Ireland for the public to read. His library became a repository for his fine collection of books to advance the minds of his host nation.

Eoin Lyons
Journalist & Author of Style Source Ireland Interiors

Niall Mullen's (105 Francis St, Dublin 8) sells spectacular Art Deco furniture. Prices are steep but it's one of my favorite shops for inspiration alone. This is dream stuff and so beautifully made. The shop has a small selection of the stock he stores in a warehouse elsewhere, so ask if you're looking for something particular. Another shop I love is Helen McAlinden's No 6 (Map p81, C2; Castle Market, Dublin 2). See her bath and bed ranges for Foxford – prices are moderate and they make great gifts. The chic interior by designer Maria MacVeigh sets off the mix of clothing, furniture and accessories. At the other end of the spectrum, the wonderful thing about Dunnes Home (Map p81, C2; S Great Georges St, Dublin 2) is that you can walk in and buy almost anything: that's a nice feeling when so many shops are prohibitively expensive. Not everything may be to your taste, but accessories such as cushions, throws, glassware and candles are so cheap they're practically disposable.

that still retains its original usage. The beautiful, dark, oak bookcases, each topped with elaborately carved and gilded gables, are filled with some 25,000 books dating from the 15th to the early 18th century.

◎ MOTHER'S TANKSHIP
☎ 671 7654; www.motherstankship .com; 41-43 Watling St; admission free; ◷ noon-6pm Thu-Sat Sep-Jun or by appointment; 🚍 51b, 78a, 123, 206; 🏛 Museum; 🚹 good
Visionary artist Finola Jones set up this factory space gallery near Guinness as an antidote to the 'safe' commercial galleries in town. New and established artists such as Gary Phelan and Ciaran Murphy show daring conceptual work.

◎ ST AUDOEN'S PROTESTANT CHURCH
☎ 677 0088; High St; admission €2.10/1.10-1.30/5.80; ◷ 9.30am-5.30pm Jun-Sep, last admission 4.45pm; 🚍 51b, 78a, 123, 206; 🚹 good
The only surviving medieval parish church in the city, St Audoen's was built between 1181 and 1212, though the site is thought to be much older. Enlarged in its 15th-century heyday, it shrank to its present size in the 18th and 19th centuries, when the eastern wing and St Anne's Chapel were

left to ruin. Today the chapel houses an excellent visitor centre, and sometimes runs guided tours.

◎ ST PATRICK'S CATHEDRAL
☎ 453 9472; www.stpatrickscathedral .ie; St Patrick's Cl; admission €5/4/12, for worshippers only during services; ◷ 9am-5pm Mon-Fri, to 5.30pm Sat, 9-11am, 12.30-2.45pm & 4.30-5.30pm Sun Mar-Oct, 9am-5pm Mon-Sat, 9-11am & 12.30-3pm Sun Nov-Feb; 🚍 49, 50, 54a, 56a, 77; 🚹 by prior arrangement
This cathedral, which is located only a mere stone's throw from its sibling Christ Church, smack-bang in the heart of old Dublin, stands where St Patrick himself is said to have baptised converts at a well – even if the story isn't exactly verifiable and the church itself in fact dates from 1191. What is proven

CATHEDRAL STRIKE
St Patrick's cathedral was the setting for a live drama that played out to massive public interest in May 2006, when 32 Afghani men (including nine minors) staged a gripping sit-in hunger strike in a bid to secure Irish asylum. It didn't work. After a week-long media flurry they came out, apologised and resumed a routine application. For a while at least, though, it put Ireland's asylum procedures on the public agenda.

KILMAINHAM & THE LIBERTIES

fact, however, is that during his 1649 'visit' to Ireland, the one and only Oliver Cromwell converted the nave into a stable for his horses.

📷 SHARKEY GALLERY
☎ 453 6282; www.kevinsharkey.com; 80 Francis St; admission free; ⏲ 11am-6pm; 🚌 51b, 78a, 121, 123; ♿ excellent

Punters enter a black room via a bulb-lit catwalk where Donegal artist and former TV presenter Kevin Sharkey's new gallery could easily pass for a '90s New York nightclub. Fans of the artist's striking abstract canvasses, which deal with issues of identity, include Bob Geldof and Charles Saatchi.

St Patrick's Cathedral (p105)

SHOP

DESIGN ASSOCIATES

☎ 453 7767; 144-145 Francis St; ⏱ 9.30am-6pm Mon-Sat; 🚌 123, 206, 51b

Choose from high-end antiques, marble statues, beautiful contemporary lamps and glass work in this tasteful interior-design shop.

FLEURY ANTIQUES

☎ 473 0878; 57 Francis St; ⏱ 9.30am-6pm Mon-Sat; 🚌 123, 206, 51b

Fleury specialises in oil paintings, vases, candelabras, silverware, porcelain and decorative pieces from the 18th century to the 1930s.

O'SULLIVAN ANTIQUES

☎ 454 1143; 43-44 Francis St; ⏱ 10am-5pm Mon-Sat; 🚌 123, 206, 51b

Specialising in fine Georgian, Victorian and Edwardian period furniture, you're also likely to come across distinctive ceramics, crystal, medals and costumes at times.

OXFAM HOME

☎ 402 0555; 86 Francis St; ⏱ 10am-5.30pm Mon-Fri, 10am-1pm Sat; 🚌 123, 206, 51b

They say charity begins at home, so get rummaging among the veneer offcuts in this furniture branch of the charity chain where you might stumble across the odd 1960s Subutio table or Art Deco dresser. Esoteric vinyl from the '80s is another speciality of the house.

DRINK

BRAZEN HEAD

☎ 679 5186; 20 Lower Bridge St; 🚌 134; ♿ to 7pm

Reputed to be Dublin's oldest pub, the Brazen Head was founded in 1198, but the present building is a young thing, dating from only 1668. Attracting foreign students and tourists as well as locals, the pub has traditional Irish music nightly, which usually kicks off around 9pm.

PLAY

VICAR STREET

☎ 454 5533; www.vicarstreet.com; 58-59 Thomas St; 🚌 51b, 78a, 123, 206

Smaller rock, folk and comedy performances take place at this venue near Christ Church Cathedral. Though it seats 1000 between its table-serviced area and theatre-style balcony, it retains an intimate atmosphere, with low lighting and an excellent sound system. Neil Young, Bob Dylan and Justin Timberlake (spot the odd one out) have all played here.

>AROUND O'CONNELL STREET

The imperially wide O'Connell St is the centre of Dublin and its most historically important thoroughfare. It became Dublin's main street in 1794, when O'Connell Bridge was built and the city's axis shifted east. The north side was the residential area of choice at the start of the Georgian period, but when the hoi polloi got too close, the aristocracy doubled back over the Liffey and settled the new areas surrounding Leinster House. Although it has lost much of its commercial and symbolic pre-eminence to Grafton St and the southside, a massive programme of urban rejuvenation has seen the grand old dame recapture some of its former grandeur, thanks in no small measure to the growing multi-ethnicity of Dublin, which has seen new arrivals bring new vitality to the surrounding streets.

AROUND O'CONNELL STREET

◉ SEE

Custom House	1	D4
Dublin City Gallery - Hugh Lane	2	B3
Dublin Writers Museum	3	A3
Garden of Remembrance	4	B3
General Post Office	5	B4
James Joyce Centre	6	B3
St Mary's Pro-Cathedral	7	C4

🛍 SHOP

Arnott's	8	B5
Connolly Books	9	B5
Dublin City Gallery - Hugh Lane Shop	(see 2)	
Dublin Woollen Mills	10	B5

Early Learning Centre	11	B4
Irish Historial Picture Company	12	B5
Jervis Centre	13	A5
Louis Copeland	14	A4
Moore Street Market	15	B4
Penney's	16	B5
Roches Stores	17	B4
Smyths Toys	18	A4
Winding Stair	(see 27)	

🍴 EAT

101 Talbot	19	C4
Chapter One	(see 3)	
Cobalt Café & Gallery	20	B3
Enoteca Delle Langhe	21	A5
Epicurean Food Hall	22	B5
La Taverna di Bacco	23	A5

Panem	24	A5
Rhodes D7	25	A5
Soup Dragon	26	A5
Winding Stair	27	B5

🍷 DRINK

Flowing Tide	28	C4
Sackville Lounge	29	C4

⭐ PLAY

Abbey Theatre	30	C5
Ambassador Theatre	31	B3
Gate Theatre	32	B3
GUBU	33	A5
Laughter Lounge	34	C5
Savoy	35	B4

SEE

CUSTOM HOUSE

☎ 888 2538; Custom House Quay; adult/child/student/family €1.30/1.30/free/3.80; ⏲ 10am-12.30pm Mon-Fri, 2-5pm Sat & Sun mid-Apr–Oct, 10am-12.30pm Wed-Fri, 2-5pm Sun Nov-Mar; 🚉 Tara Street, Connolly Station; ♿ excellent, call ahead

A breathtaking Dublin landmark, Custom House was built to house the city's tax commissioners. James Gandon's first architectural triumph, the 18th-century building (with newly cleaned façade) has a copper dome set with clock faces and neoclassical columns typical of the era. While the building now houses the Department of the Environment, the visitor centre (temporarily closed; ring for opening date) explains it's history.

DUBLIN CITY GALLERY – HUGH LANE

☎ 874 1903; www.hughlane.ie; Charlemont House, N Parnell Sq; suggested donation €2; ⏲ 9.30am-6pm Tue-Thu, to 5pm Fri-Sat, 11am-5pm Sun, guided tours 11am Tue & 1.30pm Sun; 🚌 3, 10, 16, 19, 123; 🚉 Connolly Station; ♿ limited; 👶 kids weekend workshops

Dublin City Gallery - Hugh Lane

The Hugh Lane gallery, housed in a spacious 18th-century townhouse, has been given a fantastic facelift with the unveiling of a spanking new €13-million modernist extension that more than doubles the gallery's capacity. The gallery's remit bridges the gap between the National Gallery's old masters and the cutting-edge works on show at the Irish Museum of Modern Art. One highlight is the Francis Bacon studio, painstakingly moved in all its shambolic mess from the artist's London home.

HUGH LANE HITS

> *Waterloo Bridge*, Monet
> *Parapluies*, Renoir
> *Blue and White*, William Scott
> *Sandra*, Sean Scully

DUBLIN WRITERS MUSEUM

☎ 872 2077; www.visitdublin.com; 18
N Parnell Sq; admission €6.70/5.70/19;
🕙 10am-6pm Mon-Fri, to 5pm Sat,
11am-5pm Sun Jun-Aug, 10am-5pm Mon-
Sat, 11am-5pm Sun Sep-May; 🚌 11, 13,
16, 19, 36, 40; 🚇 Connolly Station
In a house once owned by the
Jameson family (of whiskey fame),
the museum celebrates Ireland's literary history from the *Book of Kells*
onwards. In a nod to the subject
maybe, there's a mountain of text
to read on the panels, but the back
room with its quirky memorabilia –
such as Samuel Beckett's phone
and Oliver St John Gogarty's flying
goggles – offers light relief.

GARDEN OF
REMEMBRANCE

☎ 874 3074; www.heritageireland.ie;
Parnell Sq; admission free; 🕙 9.30am-
dusk May-Sep, from 11am Oct-Apr; 🚌 36,
40; 🚇 Connolly; ♿ limited

LOCATION! LOCATION!
Some say Dublin, not Leopold Bloom, is
the most important character in *Ulysses*.
Joyce claimed that if the city ever dis-
appeared, he hoped it could be recon-
structed from the detail in his book. The
story follows a single day, 16 June 1904,
in Bloom's life as he walks and rides in
trams and carriages around 30km of
Dublin streets from Dalkey to 7 Eccles St,
now site of the Mater Private Hospital.

SIGN OF THE TIMES
The provenance of a mysterious bronze
plaque on O'Connell Bridge, spotted
by a journalist, bemused the nation in
spring 2006. It commemorated a Fr Pat
Noise whose carriage had plunged into
the Liffey in 1919 in 'suspicious circum-
stances'. Even Dublin City Council were
baffled: they had no record of this man
or permission to erect any memorial.
Some art students later took credit for
the elaborate hoax but have yet to reveal their identity.

Established for the 50th anniver-
sary of the 1916 Easter Rising, this
peaceful garden commemorates
those who sacrificed their lives
in the long struggle for Irish
independence. The centrepiece is
a 1971 sculpture by Oisin Kelly de-
picting the myth of the Children
of Lir, who were turned into swans
by their wicked stepmother.

GENERAL POST OFFICE

☎ 705 7000; www.anpost.ie; Lower
O'Connell St; admission free; 🕙 8am-
8pm Mon-Sat; 🚇 O'Connell St; 🚇 Tara
Street; ♿ limited
The GPO has played a starring
role in Ireland's independence
struggles. The 1916 Easter Rising
leaders read their proclamation
of a republic from its steps – the
façade is still pockmarked from
the subsequent clash and from

NEIGHBOURHOODS

AROUND O'CONNELL STREET

fighting during the Civil War in 1922. Today the GPO still attracts protesting pressure groups and individuals on a personal crusade.

◉ JAMES JOYCE CENTRE
☎ 878 8547; www.jamesjoyce.ie; 35 N Great George's St; admission €5/4; ☷ 10am-5pm Tue-Sat; 🚌 3, 10, 11, 13, 16, 19, 22, 123; 🚇 Connolly Station

For anyone whose copy of *Ulysses* is still gathering dust on the bedside table, get to grips with the text using new user-friendly interactive displays that demystify the work. The revamped centre in a fabulous Georgian house (location of *Ulysses* dance instructor Denis Maginni's classes) explores the great scribe's life through letters and memorabilia. The centre, not to be confused with the James Joyce Museum (p133), also runs Joyce tours.

◉ ST MARY'S PRO-CATHEDRAL
☎ 874 5441; www.procathedral.ie; 83 Marlborough St; admission free; ☷ 8am-7pm Mon-Sat, 8am-2pm Sun; 🚌 27, 31b, 42a, 42b, 130; 🚇 Connolly Station

Dublin's Catholic cathedral is tucked away on Marlborough St – a deliberately inconspicuous site. Built between 1816 and 1825, the cathedral's façade is modelled on the Temple of Theseus in Athens and its carved altar is also very impressive. Oddly, Marlborough St was once the biggest red-light district in Europe…

🛍 SHOP
▢ ARNOTT'S
☎ 805 0400; Middle Abbey St; ☷ 9am-6.30pm Mon-Wed, Fri & Sat, to 9pm Thu, noon-6pm Sun; 🚌 O'Connell St; 🚇 Abbey Street

---

MONUMENTAL FAILURES

Dublin's history is littered with public monuments that have been blown up, defaced, ridiculed and bungled. William III's statue on College Green was mutilated so often it was sold for scrap in 1929, as was one of George II soon after. In 1957 Lord Gough was blown off his horse in Phoenix Park, and in 1966 Lord Nelson's head exploded onto the footpath on O'Connell St. At the north end of Grafton St, the statue of Molly Malone (Map p39, B3) with unlikely plunging neckline, represents the legendary cockles and mussels vendor who is the subject of Dublin's most famous song.

Dublin's last big civic project, the 120m-high spire sculpture, the Monument of Light (Map p109, B4) replaced Nelson's Column on O'Connell St. Heated debate about its 'purpose' delayed its scheduled erection for millennium New Year's Eve by three years, though now most Dubliners appreciate its beauty, the scorn long forgotten.

Occupying a huge block with entry on Henry, Liffey and Abbey Sts, this grand dame is one of Dublin's best department stores. From contemporary garden furniture to high fashion, it's all here, and there's a great selection of kids' designer gear on the 1st floor.

☐ CONNOLLY BOOKS
☎ 874 7981; 7 Bloom's Lane; ⏱ 10am-5.30pm Mon-Sat; 🚇 Jervis

Founded in the 1980s, this is Dublin's famous repository for radical books and political magazines. Literature on Marxism sits alongside left-wing books on Irish history, feminism and trade unionism.

☐ DUBLIN CITY GALLERY – HUGH LANE SHOP
☎ 874 1903; Charlemont House, N Parnell Sq; ⏱ 9.30am-5pm Fri & Sat, to 6pm Tue-Thu, 11am-5pm Sun; 🚌 3, 10, 16, 19, 123; 🚇 Connolly Station

You could waste some wonderful time in this almost-secret cultural playground, digging out cubist fridge magnets, huge po-mo hanging mobiles, colour-by-number masterpieces, cloth puppets, unusual wooden toys and beautiful art and pop-culture hardbacks.

☐ DUBLIN WOOLLEN MILLS
☎ 677 5014; 41 Lower Ormond Quay; ⏱ 9.30am-6pm Mon-Wed, Fri & Sat, to 7.30pm Thu, 1-6pm Sun; 🚌 all cross-city; 🚇 Jervis

Situated at the northern end of Ha'penny Bridge, this is one of Dublin's major wool outlets. It features a large selection of traditional sweaters, cardigans, scarves, rugs, shawls and other woollen goods, and runs a tax-free shopping scheme.

☐ EARLY LEARNING CENTRE
☎ 873 1945; 3 Henry St; ⏱ 9am-5pm Mon-Wed, Fri & Sat, to 8pm Thu, to 5.30pm Sat, 1-5pm Sun; 🚌 all cross-city; 🚇 Jervis

Fun with an educational bent for the tiniest tots, including ELC-brand plastic and wooden toys, spelling and numerical games, simple devices that honk and squeak and a good range of Thomas the Tank Engine stuff.

☐ IRISH HISTORICAL PICTURE COMPANY
☎ 872 0144; 5 Lower Ormond Quay; ⏱ 9am-6pm Mon-Fri, 10am-5pm Sat & Sun; 🚌 all cross-city; 🚇 Jervis

With a print collection that's second only to the holdings at the National Library, this place has more than 12,000 pictures taken around Ireland at the turn of the 20th century. The prints cover all 32 counties and range from town streetscapes to images of bog cutters. Mounted prints can be framed within minutes.

🏠 JERVIS CENTRE
☎ 878 1323; Jervis St; ⏰ 9am-6pm Mon-Wed, Fri & Sat, to 9pm Thu, noon-6pm Sun; 🚇 Jervis

An ultramodern, domed mall that's a veritable shrine to the British chain store. Boots, Top Shop, Debenhams, Argos, Dixons, M&S and Miss Selfridge all get a look-in.

🏠 LOUIS COPELAND
☎ 872 1600; 39-41 Capel St; ⏰ 9am-5.30pm Mon-Sat, to 7.30pm Thu; 🚌 37, 70, 134, 172; 🚇 Jervis

A Dublin tradition for off-the-peg suits and casual menswear, with Lacoste, Burberry, Dior and Louis Ferraud. Louis himself works at the original Capel St store; there are two others including one at 18–19 Wicklow St (Map p39, A3).

🏠 MOORE STREET MARKET
Moore St; ⏰ 9am-4pm Mon-Sat; 🚌 all cross-city; 🚇 Jervis

An open-air, steadfastly 'Old Dublin' market, with fruit, fish and flowers on offer. Traditional vendors hawk cheap cigarettes, tobacco and chocolate among the new wave of Chinese and Nigerians selling phone cards and hair

Moore Street Market

extensions. Don't try to buy just one banana though – if the sign says 10 for €1, that's what it is.

 PENNEY'S

☎ 872 0466; 37 O'Connell St; ⊗ 8.30am-6.30pm Mon-Sat, to 9pm Thu, noon-6pm Sun; 🚊 O'Connell St; 🚇 Abbey Street

The clothes might not withstand industrial washing but who cares when they only cost €3? Penney's attraction is its bright up-to-the-minute tops, funky underwear and knits for adults and juniors.

ROCHES STORES

☎ 873 0044; 83 Henry St; ⊗ 9am-6.30pm Mon-Wed, Fri & Sat, to 9pm Thu, noon-6pm Sun; 🚊 O'Connell St; 🚇 Jervis

New-look Roches is a modern department store at its shiny best – bold and glass-fronted on the outside and street-smart fashion labels such as Zara, Warehouse and G-Star on the inside, as well as the obligatory homewares and electrical sections.

SMYTHS TOYS

☎ 878 2878; Jervis St; ⊗ 10am-6pm Mon-Wed, Fri & Sat, to 9pm Thu, 1-6pm Sun; 🚊 all cross-city; 🚇 Jervis

Relive your childhood in this toy superstore, with towering aisles full of Barbies, Lego, V-Tech, various action men, soft toys, puzzles, board and electronic games and

Winding Stair

a whole room devoted to Play-stations, Gameboys and DVDs.

WINDING STAIR

☎ 873 3292; 40 Lower Ormond Quay; ⊗ 9.30am-6pm Mon-Sat; 🚊 all cross-city; 🚇 Jervis

There was a public outcry when this creaky old place closed a few years ago. It's just reopened its doors and Dublin's bohemians, students and literati can once more thumb the fine selection of new and second-hand books crammed into heaving bookcases. When you've had enough of browsing, head up the winding stairs to the excellent café (p118).

Epicurean Food Hall

🍴 EAT

🍴 101 TALBOT

Mediterranean/Middle Eastern €€

☎ 874 5011; 101 Talbot St; 🕑 5-11pm Tue-Sat; 🚌 all cross-city; ♿ Ⓥ

Funky 101 Talbot is a perennial favourite of artists, students, locals and theatre-goers. They're attracted by its eclectic menu, canteen-style atmosphere and artwork. Its scallops with black pudding and raspberry dressing are divine.

🍴 CHAPTER ONE

European €€€€

☎ 873 2266; 18-19 Parnell Sq; 🕑 12.30-2.30pm & 6-11pm Tue-Sat; 🚌 10, 11, 16, 19; ♿ Ⓥ

It's a wonder Ross Lewis' cooking hasn't been recognised by Michelin yet but maybe it doesn't travel north of the Liffey. Enjoy rack of lamb with mint purée, John Dory with tomato caper compote or rabbit with morel fricasée with excellent service in an unstuffy atmosphere. The pre-theatre menu is popular for its great value.

🍴 COBALT CAFÉ & GALLERY

Café €

☎ 873 0313; 16 N Great George's St; 🕑 10am-4.30pm Mon-Fri; 🚌 all cross-city; ♿ Ⓥ

This gorgeous, elegant café housed in a bright and airy Georgian drawing room is a must, if you're in the 'hood. Almost opposite the James Joyce Centre, the menu is simple but you'll relish hearty soups by a roaring fire in winter or bouncy fresh sandwiches and salads in the garden on warmer days.

🍴 EPICUREAN FOOD HALL

Food hall €

Lower Liffey St; 🕑 9.30am-5.30pm Mon-Sat; 🚌 all cross-city; Ⓜ Jervis; ♿ ♿ Ⓥ

Need to refuel and rest the bag-laden arms? Then this busy arcade with 20-odd food stalls is just the ticket. Quality is hit and miss, but you won't go wrong with a hot bagel from Itsabagel or finger-licking kebab from Istanbul House rounded off with an espresso from the excellent El Corte.

🍴 LA TAVERNA DI BACCO
Italian €€

☎ 873 0040; 24 Lower Ormond Quay; ⏰ 12.30-10.30pm Tue-Sat, from 5pm Sun; 🚌 all cross-city; 🚊 Jervis; ♿ 👶 Ⓥ

Football-mad developer Mick Wallace has managed to single-handedly create a thriving new Italian quarter with cafés and eateries popping up all over Quartier Bloom, the new lane from Ormond Quay to Great Strand St. La Taverna and **Enoteca Delle Langhe** (☎ 888 0834, Bloom's Lane) a few doors up serve simple pastas, antipasti and Italian cheeses, along with the delicious produce of his own vineyard and others in Piemonte.

🍴 PANEM *Café* €

☎ 872 8510; 21 Lower Ormond Quay; ⏰ 9am-5.30pm Mon-Sat; 🚌 all cross-city; 🚊 Jervis; 👶 Ⓥ

Pass this tiny café (there's only room for six to sit) and you'll be lured in by the aroma of fresh *pains au chocolat* (chocolate croissant), savoury focaccias, almond pastries and 100%

Arabica Torrisi coffee from Sicily. Mmmm…and you won't find much cheaper in Dublin.

🍴 RHODES D7 *British* €€€

☎ 804 4441; Mary's Abbey; ⏰ noon-10pm Tue-Sat, to 4pm Sun & Mon; 🚊 Jervis; ♿ 👶 🚊 Ⓥ

Is Ireland ready for a truly British restaurant? Celebrity-TV chef and Londoner Gary Rhodes thinks so, with the opening of his big, brash northside eaterie. While you won't spot the Tintin-haired one sweating it out in the kitchen, he did devise the menu and his British staples – cheddar rarebit, roast cod with lobster champ – have been given an Irish twist.

🍴 SOUP DRAGON
Soups & breakfast €

☎ 872 3277; 168 Capel St; ⏰ 8am-4pm Mon-Fri, 11am-5pm Sat; 👶 Ⓥ

Eat in or takeaway one of 13 tasty homemade soups, including Thai Green Curry or fish chowder in full

---

NO SMOKE WITHOUT IRE

Since the smoking ban in all public places took effect at the end of March 2004, those who once enjoyed a postprandial toke at the table must now – rain or shine – satisfy their nicotine hit outdoors. By nifty consequence, restaurant and bar smoking areas have become the best pick-up joints in town, as strangers share a quiet corner over a smoke.

---

or low-fat options. Bowls come in three different sizes and prices include homemade bread and a piece of fruit. Kick-start your day with a healthy all-day breakfast selection: fresh smoothies, generous bowls of yogurt, fruit and muesli or poached egg in a bagel.

🍴 WINDING STAIR *Irish* €€€

☎ 873 3292; 40 Lower Ormond Quay; 🕙 9am-6pm Mon-Sat, from 1pm Sun; 🚻 Ⓥ

There was much tearing of hair and gnashing of teeth when this Dublin institution closed two years ago. Thankfully it reopened in 2006 with the same simple décor and warm atmosphere but with the addition of an excellent wine list and Irish menu – creamy fish pie, bacon and organic cabbage, steamed mussels or Irish farmyard cheeses – all prepared with TLC.

🍸 DRINK
🍸 FLOWING TIDE

☎ 874 0842; 9 Lower Abbey St; 🚌 all cross-city; 🚇 Abbey Street; 🚻 to 7pm

Directly opposite the Abbey Theatre, the Flowing Tide attracts a great mix of theatre-goers, northside locals and the odd thespian downing a quick one between rehearsals. It's loud, full of chat and a great place to drink. What more could you ask for in a pub?

🍸 SACKVILLE LOUNGE

☎ 874 5222; Sackville Pl; 🚌 all cross-city; 🚇 Abbey Street; 🚻 to 7pm

This tiny 19th-century one-room, wood-panelled bar is discreetly located just off O'Connell St, which perhaps explains why it's so popular with actors, theatre-goers and anyone who appreciates a nice pint in a gorgeous old-style bar.

⭐ PLAY
⭐ ABBEY THEATRE

☎ 878 7222; www.abbeytheatre.ie; Lower Abbey St; admission Abbey Theatre €12-30, Peacock Theatre €10-18; 🕙 box office 10.30am-7pm Mon-Sat; 🚌 all cross-city; 🚇 Abbey Street; ♿ good in Abbey, none in Peacock; 🚻

Together with the more experimental Peacock Theatre on the same premises, the Abbey is Ireland's national theatre. The theatre shows work by established contemporary Irish writers as well as classics by WB Yeats, JM Synge, Sean O'Casey and Samuel Beckett. At the Peacock works tend to be by young writers and performed by less-established actors. See also p19.

⭐ AMBASSADOR THEATRE

www.mcd.ie; Upper O'Connell St; 🕙 doors open 7.30pm; 🚌 all cross-city

This former cinema, at the top of O'Connell St, has thankfully kept much of its rococo interior intact. The view of its international acts on stage is better from the spacious downstairs auditorium, while on the mezzanine level it's seating only in old velvet cinema seats, complete with drinks holders.

⭐ GATE THEATRE
☎ 874 4045; www.gate-theatre.ie; E Parnell Sq; admission €15-30; 🕒 box office 10am-7pm Mon-Sat; 🚌 all cross-city
International classics from the likes of Harold Pinter and Noel Coward, older Irish works by playwrights such as Oscar Wilde, George Bernard Shaw and Oliver Goldsmith, as well as newer plays are performed here. See also p19.

⭐ GUBU
☎ 874 0710; Capel St; 🕒 4-11.30pm, to 12.30am Thu-Sat; 🚌 37, 70, 134, 172; 🚆 Jervis
The northside's best gay-and-lesbian bar, 'Gaybu' is a stylish spot with stressed metal and chunky furniture. Wednesday's comedy night with Busty Lycra and Thursday's Stars Come Out audiovisual show are popular.

⭐ LAUGHTER LOUNGE
☎ 1800 266 339; Eden Quay; admission €20; 🕒 shows start 9pm Thu-Sat; 🚌 all cross-city; 🚆 Abbey Street; ♿ good
Dublin's only purpose-built comedy venue can squeeze 400

Ha'penny bridge

punters in for live shows, which feature four high-quality Irish and international acts each night. Admission includes entry to the postcomedy clubs.

⭐ SAVOY
☎ 874 6000; Upper O'Connell St; tickets before/after 6pm €6.50/8.50; 🕒 2-11pm; 🚌 all cross-city; 🚆 Abbey Street; ♿
A traditional old-style six-screen, first-run cinema for general releases with late-night shows at weekends. The big-screen one is Ireland's largest.

>SMITHFIELD & PHOENIX PARK

An area very much in development, Smithfield promises to be cool and sophisticated, with new designer buildings surrounding a sexy square that will provide a meeting point for the trendy young things that shop, eat, drink and live nearby. It is happening, but it's not quite there. The main square, now the centrepiece of the new development, has been synonymous with markets since the 17th century and, in recent decades, scene of a bustling horse fair where deals were sealed with a spit in your hand. All gone now, hurriedly moved on because fruit 'n' veg and hoof inspections didn't fit the planned aesthetic. The 400,000-odd antique cobblestones that saw their share of horse manure over the decades were removed, hand-cleaned and relaid alongside new granite slabs, giving the square a brand new look. Further on up the Liffey is Phoenix Park, the giant green lung that is the city's biggest playground.

SMITHFIELD & PHOENIX PARK

☉ SEE
Chimney 1 F5
Dublin Zoo 2 A3
Four Courts 3 G5
Kevin Kavanagh Gallery .. 4 H5
National Museum of
Ireland - Decorative Arts
& History 5 E5

Old Jameson Distillery ... 6 F5
Phoenix Park 7 A4
St Michan's Church 8 G5

John M Keating 12 H5
Voodoo Lounge 13 F5

▼ DRINK
Cobblestone 9 F4
Dice Bar 10 F5
Hughes' Bar 11 G5

Please see over for map

SEE

CHIMNEY

☎ 817 3838; Smithfield Village; admission €5/3.50; ⏱ 10am-5pm Mon-Sat, 10.30am-5.30pm Sun; 🚌 67, 67a, 68, 69, 79, 134; 🚃 Smithfield

Re-live Willy Wonka's final scene by shuttling up a 56m glass lift to Dublin's first and only 360-degree observation tower. OK, so you don't burst into Pinewood Studios, but on a clear day you can view the entire city, the ocean and the mountains to the south all from the comfort of this converted 1895 Jameson distillery chimney.

DUBLIN ZOO

☎ 677 1425; www.dublinzoo.ie; Phoenix Park; admission €13.50/6.30-9/38; ⏱ 9.30am-6pm Mon-Sat, 10.30am-6pm Sun May-Sep, 9.30am-4pm Mon-Fri, 9.30am-5pm Sat, 10.30am-5pm Sun Oct-Apr; 🚌 10 from O'Connell St, 25 or 26 from Abbey St Middle; 🚻 good

The second-oldest public zoo in Europe, the Dublin Zoo calls itself home to more than 700 animals, including rhinos, gorillas, leopards, penguins and polar bears. Apart from the animal antics, children will enjoy the regular feedings, the minitrain ride through the zoo grounds, the African safari plains and, if all else fails, the big playground.

Chimney

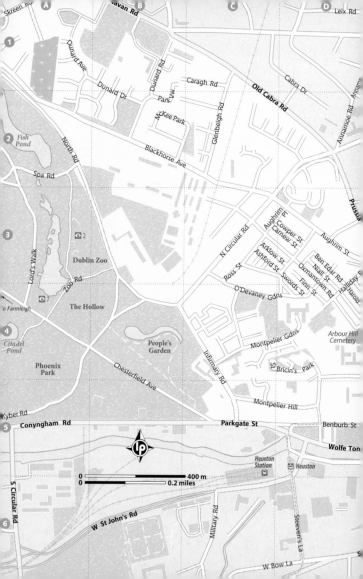

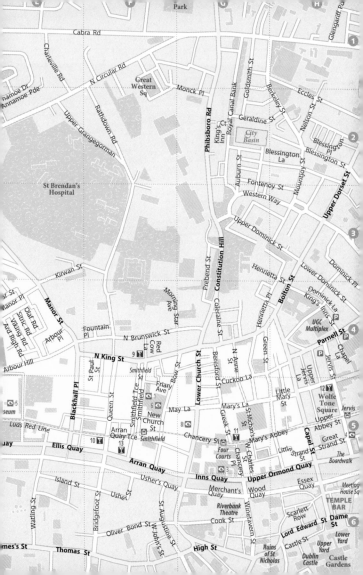

Rotunda of the Four Courts

◎ FARMLEIGH

☎ 815 5900; www.farmleigh.ie;
Phoenix Park, Castleknock; admission free;
◷ 10.30am-5.30pm Sat & Sun, call ahead,
may be closed for official events; 🚌 37
from city centre; ♿ excellent, call ahead
Another splendid feather in
architect James Gandon's cap, this
fine Georgian-Victorian pile, once
part of the Guinness estate, was
restored to immaculate standard by
the state in 2001. Only the ground
floor, with a fantastic library and
glass conservatory, is on view but
the vast pleasure gardens with lake,
walled and Japanese gardens are a
delight to stroll. It is the apt setting

for the RTE Summer Proms, a series
of free popular classical concerts
with guest conductors during July.

◎ FOUR COURTS

☎ 888 6441; Inns Quay; admission
free; ◷ 9am-4.30pm Mon-Fri; 🚌 134;
🚇 Four Courts; ♿ good
With its 130m-long façade and
neoclassical proportions, the Four
Courts was built between 1786
and 1802 to the design of James
Gandon. In 1922 the building was
captured by anti-Treaty republi-
cans, and pro-Treaty forces shelled
the site to try to dislodge them.
Displays on the building's history

and reconstruction are on the 1st floor. Court hearings can be observed from public galleries between 10am and 4pm only.

KEVIN KAVANAGH GALLERY

☎ 874 0064; www.kevinkavanaghgallery.ie; 66 Great Strand St; admission free; ☺ 10am-5pm Tue-Sat, 11am-4pm Sat; 🚍 37, 70, 134, 172; 🚈 Jervis; ♿ good

On a backstreet behind the Morrison Hotel, Kevin Kavanagh's intimate gallery has a reputation of unearthing emerging Dublin artists, many of whom now show at Irish Museum of Modern Art (IMMA) and abroad. Catch them here first.

NATIONAL MUSEUM OF IRELAND – DECORATIVE ARTS & HISTORY

☎ 677 7444; www.museum.ie; Benburb St; admission free; ☺ 10am-5pm Tue-Sat, from 2pm Sun, free daily tours at 3.30pm; 🚍 25, 25a, 66, 67, 90, 92; 🚈 Museum; ♿ excellent; 👶 special events & educational workshops for kids held regularly

Once the world's largest military barracks (named after Michael Collins), this splendid early neoclassical greystone building on the Liffey's northern banks is now home to the Decorative Arts & History collection of the National Museum of Ireland. Inside the imposing exterior lies a treasure

trove of artefacts ranging from silver, ceramics and glassware to weaponry, furniture and folk-life displays. Don't miss the Fonthill vase; Lord Chancellor's mace; Domville doll's house; and Eugene Rosseau's carp vase.

OLD JAMESON DISTILLERY

☎ 807 2355; Bow St, Smithfield; admission €8.75/3.95-7/21; ☺ 9.30am-5.30pm, by tour only; 🚍 67, 67a, 68, 69, 79, 134; 🚈 Smithfield; ♿ good

Housed in the original Jameson distillery where the famous Irish whiskey was produced from 1791 to 1966, the museum tells the story of the site and the drink. A heavy dose of marketing is thrown in, but fans will enjoy the re-created old factory, detailed explanations of the distilling process and, of course, the free glass of Jameson at the end of the tour.

PHOENIX PARK

☎ 677 0095; www.opw.ie; park grounds free, visitor centre admission €2.90/1.30-2.10/7.40; ☺ visitor centre 10am-6pm Jun-Sep, 10am-5pm Oct, 9.30am-4.30pm Nov-Mar, 9.30am-5.30pm Apr & May, free 1hr tours of president's residence depart visitor centre 10.30am-4pm Sat; 🚍 visitor centre 37, 38, 39, park gate 10, 25, 26, 66, 67 68, 69; ♿ good

One of the world's largest city parks is where you'll find iPod-clad joggers, grannies pushing

MURDER IN THE PARK

In 1882 Lord Cavendish, British chief secretary for Ireland, and his assistant were stabbed to death in Phoenix Park by members of a Fenian splinter nationalist group called The Invincibles. The assassins escaped but one of their comrades betrayed them and they were hanged at Kilmainham Gaol.

buggies, ladies walking poodles, gardens, lakes, a sporting ground and 300 deer. There are also cricket and polo grounds, a motor-racing track and some fine 18th-century residences, including those of the Irish president and the US ambassador.

◯ ST MICHAN'S CHURCH

☎ 872 4154; Lower Church St; admission €3.50/3; 🕙 10am-12.45pm & 2-4.30pm Mon-Fri Apr-Oct, 12.30pm-3.30pm Mon-Fri Nov-Mar, 10am-12.45pm Sat; 🚍 134; 🚻 limited

Founded by Danes in 1095, major rebuilding in 1686 and 1828 left little of the original church here. The church has a fine oak organ that may have been played by Handel, but the star attraction is the underground vault, where buried bodies have been gruesomely mummified by the magnesium limestone walls, limbs bursting out of coffins.

🍸 DRINK

🍸 COBBLESTONE

☎ 872 1799; 77 N King St; admission €8-12; 🚍 134; 🚇 Smithfield

Bordering Smithfield Sq, this great old spit-on-the-floor bar is Pixies' Frank Black's favourite hangout when he's in town. A great bunch of rising stars and tried-and-tested old hands of the trad scene play sessions here nightly till everyone's turfed out the door.

🍸 DICE BAR

☎ 674 6710; 79 Queen St; 🚍 25, 37, 39, 79, 90; 🚇 Smithfield

Co-owned by singer Huey from the Fun Lovin' Criminals, the Dice Bar looks like something you'd expect to find on New York's Lower East Side. Its black-and-red painted interior and dripping candles make it a magnet for Dublin's beautiful beatnik crowds. Pull up in your Thunderbird for Teddy Boy rockabilly night on Sunday.

🍸 HUGHES' BAR

☎ 872 6540; 19 Chancery St; 🚍 all cross-city; 🚇 Four Courts; 🚻 to 7pm

By day this pub is popular with barristers and their clients from the nearby Four Courts, and the early opening hours caters for the workers from the market across the street. But by night the place transforms into a traditional music venue, where you'll hear some

Hughes' Bar

skilled session players put their instruments to work.

Y JOHN M KEATING
☎ 878 0223; Mary St; ☽ 10am-1am Mon-Wed, to 2.30am Thu-Sat, 12.30pm-midnight Sun; 🚇 Jervis; ♿ good; 🚶
We don't normally go in for Superpubs but this one deserves a mention. Irish patriot Wolfe Tone, who was baptised here, and Arthur Guinness, brewery founder, who married here, might have conflicting views on the fate of this remarkable early-18th-century church. The glorious restoration features an enormous organ and

historically important wall plaques and inscriptions. Expect a well-heeled crowd.

Y VOODOO LOUNGE
☎ 873 6013; 37 Arran Quay; ☽ 12.30-11.30pm Mon-Wed, to 2.30am Thu-Sat, 12.30-11pm Sun; 🚌 25, 37, 39, 79, 90; 🚇 Smithfield
Run by the same crew as Dice Bar (opposite), Voodoo Lounge, on the quays just south of Smithfield, is a long, dark bar with decadent, Gothic Louisiana–style décor. Indie, electropop and rock music are played loud, and that's the way the fun-lovin' crowd likes it.

>BEYOND THE GRAND CANAL

Dublin's wealthiest suburbs are laid out south of the Grand Canal, which marks the city centre's southern boundary. These include the much sought-after postcode of Dublin 4, a byword for posh sophistication and privilege that everyone not from there likes to envy and poke fun at. It has some nice things to see too.

Built to connect Dublin with the River Shannon in the centre of Ireland, the Grand Canal makes a graceful 6km loop around south Dublin and enters the Liffey at Ringsend, through locks that were built in 1796. The large Grand Canal Dock, flanked by Hanover and Charlotte Quays, is now used by windsurfers and canoeists and is the site of major new development.

BEYOND THE GRAND CANAL

⊙ SEE
Helen Dillon's
Garden............................. 1 B5
Herbert Park.................... 2 D4

🍴 EAT
Diep Noodle Bar 3 A5
Expresso Bar..................... 4 C3
French Paradox 5 D3
Itsa4 .... 6 F3
Mint Screen 7 A5
Ocean................................ 8 D1
Roly's Bistro 9 D4
Tribeca............................. 10 B5

★ PLAY
RDS Concert Hall 11 E4
Shelbourne Greyhound
Stadium.......................... 12 D1

Please see over for map

◉ SEE

◉ AIRFIELD TRUST GARDENS
☎ 298 4301; www.airfield.ie; Upper Kilmacud Rd, Dundrum; admission €5/4/3; ☾ 10am-4pm Tue-Sat, 11am-4pm Sun; 🚌 44, 46a, 48a; ⛨ good

Once the home of eccentric philanthropist sisters Letitia and Naomi Overend, the Airfield estate is now held in trust for public use. Though the house is closed to the public (except for the excellent café) the lovely 16-hectare grounds with walled gardens, pet farm, vintage car museum and medicinal garden are great for a stroll.

◉ HELEN DILLON'S GARDEN
☎ 497 1308; 45 Sandford Rd, Ranelagh; admission €5; ☾ 2-6pm Mar, Jul & Aug, 2-6pm Sun Apr-Jun & Sep; 🚌 11, 13; 🚇 Cowper; ⛨ not allowed

Gardening enthusiasts will enjoy a visit to award-winning gardener Helen Dillon's own dramatic garden at her 1830s home. Inspired by Granada's Alhambra, the walled garden is inventively landscaped with an impressive canal feature and colour-coded exotic borders.

◉ HERBERT PARK
Ballsbridge; admission free; ☾ dawn-dusk; 🚌 5, 7, 7a, 8, 45, 46; 🚇 Sandymount, Lansdowne Road; ⛨ good

A gorgeous swathe of green lawns, ponds and flower beds

Boating on the Grand Canal

DUBLIN'S CANALS
True Dubliners, it is said, are born within the confines of the two canals, the Grand and Royal, that encircle the inner city. Thanks to the vision of the Wide Street Commission who, nearly a quarter of a century ago, restricted building closer than 32m to the water, the tree-lined canal paths have become an amenity enjoyed by Dubliners. An evening barge trip is an atmospheric way to experience the canals. Board **La Peniche** (☎ 087 790 0077; Grand Canal, Mespil Rd; ☾ 8.30-10.30pm Thu), sit on deck and enjoy fine wine and food while your skipper navigates the locks.

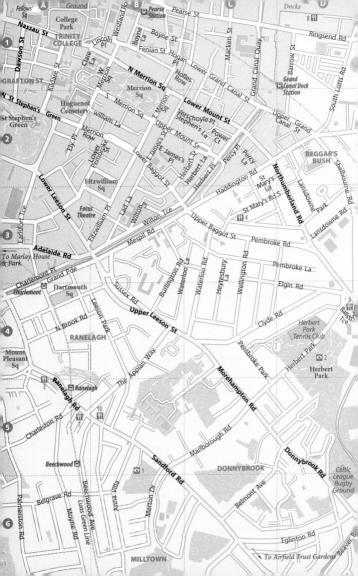

Orla Barry
Broadcaster, Newstalk

I live in the southern suburb of Ranelagh, and it's my favourite place to go for breakfast. The nicest cafés transport me to another place, far from Dublin, and I like to mind-travel with big mugs of coffee and the newspapers. On Saturdays, I like to potter about the city centre, exploring the markets of Temple Bar like the Cow's Lane Market (p70) and the food market on Meeting House Square (p71). I don't usually buy anything, but it's fun to browse. The café in Avoca Handweavers (p42) is one of my favourites, for the food and the atmosphere, as is the lovely Honest to Goodness (p90) in the George's St Arcade – they do fabulous sandwiches. After lunch I like to potter a bit more, maybe take a trip out to the Irish Museum of Modern Art in Kilmainham, but more often than not I have a look at what's on in the Screen (p51), the best of the city-centre cinemas – I hate the big multiplexes; too many queues, too impersonal.

near the Royal Dublin Society Showgrounds. Sandwiched between prosperous Ballsbridge and Donnybrook, the park runs along the River Dodder. There are tennis courts and a kids' playground here too.

JAMES JOYCE MUSEUM

☎ 280 9265; Martello tower, Sandycove; admission €6.70/4.20-5.70/18; ⏱ 10am-1pm & 2-5pm Mon-Sat, 2-6pm Sun & holidays Apr-Oct, by arrangement only Nov-Mar, open 8am-6pm Bloomsday (16 Jun) with special events; 🚌 59 from Dun Laoghaire; 🚉 Sandycove & Glasthule; ♿ limited

Strikingly located in a Martello tower overlooking Dublin Bay in the salubrious seaside suburb of Sandycove, the museum's contents combine memorabilia from the celebrated writer's life with a dramatic setting that has a story all its own. The opening scene of *Ulysses* is set on the tower's roof.

FORTY FOOT SWIM

Just below the Martello tower is the Forty Foot Pool. At the close of the first chapter of *Ulysses*, Buck Mulligan heads to the pool for a morning swim, an activity which is still a local tradition. For years the spot was reserved for male-only nude bathing, but women are now allowed. Though a sign warns that 'togs must be worn', die-hard men still keep the tradition up before 9am.

MARLAY HOUSE & PARK

Grange Rd, Rathfarnham; admission free; ⏱ 10am-dusk; 🚌 15c, 16, 16a, 48; ♿ good

Marlay Park, 9km south of the city centre, is a wonderful 83-hectare open space, with 17th-century buildings, wooded area, abundant wildlife, walled garden, sculpture trail and craft centre. Kids will especially love the fairy bridge, massive playground, skateboard park and, in summer, the minitrain (3pm to 5pm May to September) that jostles around a field track.

🛍 SHOP

🏬 BLACKROCK MARKET

Main St, Blackrock; ⏱ 11am-5.30pm Sat, from 10am Sun; 🚉 Blackrock

The long-running atmospheric Blackrock Market tumbles out of an old merchant house and yard in this seaside village. It has all manner of stalls selling everything from New Age crystals and dodgy Dollar albums to futons and piping-hot French waffles.

🍴 EAT

🍴 DIEP NOODLE BAR Asian €€

☎ 497 6550; Ranelagh; ⏱ 5.30-10.30pm Mon, 12.30-11pm Tue-Fri, 3-11pm Sat & Sun; 🚌 11, 11a, 13b; 🚉 Ranelagh; ♿ 🍼 Ⓥ

Top-notch Thai and Vietnamese dishes such as *pad thai* (Thai fried

NEIGHBOURHOODS

BEYOND THE GRAND CANAL

WORTH THE TRIP: DALKEY

Handsome Dalkey lies about 13km south of the city centre, a trendy and desirable village full of pubs, restaurants and – increasingly – Dublin's well-to-do.

The roofless **Archibold's Castle** on Castle St is closed except at Christmas, when a nativity crib is open to visitors. Across the road is the 15th-century **Dalkey Castle Heritage Centre**, which houses an interesting **visitor centre** (☎ 285 8366; admission €6/5/16; ☼ 9.30am-5pm Mon-Fri, from 11am Sat, Sun & hol). Exhibits explain the castle's defence systems, the history of the area's transport and various myths and legends. The Living History tour at weekends includes a re-enactment of medieval Dublin. The remains of the 11th-century **St Begnet's church & graveyard** are also here.

The waters around **Dalkey Island** are popular with scuba divers – catch one of the small boats touting for business at Coliemore Harbour. To get to Dalkey from Dublin, catch the DART (see p168).

noodles), red snapper vermicelli or seafood rice noodles come to your table at lightning speed in this funky place. Décor is sparse, modern and clean. It's packed at weekends but you'll get a table early or late without a booking.

🍴 EXPRESSO BAR *Café*   €€€
☎ 660 0585; 1 St Mary's Rd; ☼ 7.30am-5pm Mon, to 9pm Tue-Fri, 9am-4.30pm & 6-9pm Sat, 10am-4.30pm Sun; 🚌 10; ♿ ♨ Ⓥ
Hidden away on a leafy suburban road off Baggot St, this hip, minimalist place with leather seating and subdued lighting attracts local rock stars and other types normally seen only in the social columns. Top nosh such as lamb shank or baked sea bass with lime-and-mint potatoes should keep most folk happy when they're not people-watching over *Hello!* magazine.

🍴 FRENCH PARADOX
French   €€
☎ 660 4068; 53 Shelbourne Rd; ☼ noon-3pm & 5-10pm Mon-Sat, noon-4pm Sun; 🚌 5, 7, 7a, 8, 45, 46
This bright and airy wine bar over an excellent wine shop of the same name serves fine authentic French dishes such as cassoulet, a variety of foie gras, cheese and charcuterie plates, and large green salads. All there to complement the main attraction: a dazzling array of fine wines, mostly French unsurprisingly, sold by the bottle, glass or even 6.25cL taste! A little slice of Paris in Dublin.

🍴 ITSA4 *Modern Irish*   €€
☎ 219 4676; Sandymount Green; ☼ 11am-4pm & 6-10pm Mon-Fri, from 10am Sat, noon-8pm Sun; 🚉 Sandymount; ♿ ♨ excellent; Ⓥ

While Itsa4's funky flamboyant interior has been used for many fashion shoots, organic chef and writer Domini Kemp is far from frivolous. Her latest venture continues her ambitions to deliver well-sourced, quality food in delicious, down-to-earth ways. Lamb shank with lyonnaise potatoes or chicory, blue cheese and glazed pear salad are incredible. Serious food for fun people.

MINT SCREEN European €€€

☎ 497 8655; 47 Ranelagh Rd; ⏰ noon-3pm & 6-10pm; 🚌 11, 11a, 13b; 🚆 Ranelagh; ♿

The people at Mint are ambitious. Chef Oliver Dunne crossed the water from Gordon Ramsay's Pied à Terre in London and his diverse menu has 'Michelin Aspirant' written all over it. The small room is sleek and low-lit, the service formal but friendly. Expect classics such as

Students taking their lunch break near the Grand Canal

veal on foie gras, mushroom risotto or mallard duck confit.

🍴 OCEAN Seafood   €€

☎ 668 8862; Charlotte Quay Dock; ⏱ noon-11pm Mon-Fri, to 1.30am Sat, 12.30-11pm Sun (kitchen closes 10pm); 🚌 all cross-city; ♿ 🚼 Ⓥ

Popular with local business folk, this is a trendy, minimalist place with big windows overlooking the water (and trendy Hanover Quay, where U2's new recording studio will be built). There are plenty of outdoor seats from which to savour oysters, crab cakes or a variety of wraps.

🍴 ROLY'S BISTRO
Traditional Irish   €€€

☎ 668 2611; 7 Ballsbridge Tce; ⏱ noon-2.45pm & 6-9.45pm; 🚌 5, 7, 7a, 8, 45, 46

Roly's is an institution with Dublin's business fraternity (the *Daily Mail* is based beside it). It's always packed and serves up reliably good nosh. The menu is confidently traditional; fish and chips with mushy peas or sage-and-sausage-stuffed chicken, but most people come for the hobnobbing.

🍴 TRIBECA Brasserie   €€

☎ 497 4174; 65 Ranelagh Rd; ⏱ noon-11pm; 🚌 11, 11a, 13b; 🚆 Ranelagh; 🚼 Ⓥ

This New York–style brasserie has been packed since it opened and

runs a waiting list from 5pm. So what's the big deal? Legendary burgers, cobb salad with blue cheese dressing and Clonakilty black pudding omelettes eaten in a funky interior adorned with photos of cabs, politicians and rabbis.

⭐ PLAY

☆ COMHALTAS CEOLTÓ IRI ÉIREANN

☎ 280 0295; www.comhaltas.com; 35 Belgrave Sq, Monkstown; show or céilidh €10; ⏱ 9pm-midnight Mon-Sat; 🚌 7, 7a, 8 from Trinity College; 🚆 Seapoint

Serious aficionados of traditional music should make the trip here. The name (*col*-tas kyohl-*thory* erin) means 'Fraternity of Traditional Musicians of Ireland'. Here you'll find the best Irish music and dancing in Dublin, with some of the country's top players. There are nightly shows but the 'craic is mighty' at Friday night's *céilidh* (group Irish dance). See also p22.

☆ ROYAL DUBLIN SOCIETY CONCERT HALL

☎ 668 0866; Ballsbridge; www.rds.ie; 🚌 5, 7, 7a, 8, 45; 🚆 Sandymount; ♿ good; 🚼

The huge concert hall at the RDS Showgrounds hosts a rich, varied programme of classical music and opera throughout the year, with Irish and international performers.

Bookmaker at Shelbourne Greyhound Stadium

⭐ SHELBOURNE GREYHOUND STADIUM

☎ 668 3502; www.shelbournepark.com; South Lotts Rd; admission €10; ⏰ 7-10.30pm Wed, Thu & Sat; 🚍 3, 7, 7A, 8, 45 & 84 from Trinity College

All the comforts, including a restaurant overlooking the track, make going to the dogs one of the best nights out around. Table service (including betting) means that you don't even have to get out of your seat. See also p20.

>BEYOND THE ROYAL CANAL

Go north, past the Royal Canal, to discover not just a bunch of traditional suburbs but some of the more interesting sights and attractions in the city, including one of the best museums and one of the quirkiest, most handsome buildings. A little further on, about 5.6km northwest of central Dublin, the outlying suburb of Glasnevin is home to two diverse historic sights that are just perfect for a relaxed afternoon ramble. The area is dominated by the mighty Croke Park, headquarters of Gaelic games. There are also a host of compelling sights, including the architecturally magnificent Casino at Marino, the historic Prospect Cemetery and the soothing National Botanic Gardens.

Royal Canal

SEE

CASINO AT MARINO

☎ 833 1618; www.heritageireland
.ie; Malahide Rd, Marino; admission
€2.90/1.30-2.10/7.40; ⏰ 10am-6pm
Jun-Sep, to 5pm May & Oct, noon-4pm
Sat & Sun Nov-Dec & Feb-Apr (to 5pm
Apr), last tour 45min before closing;
🚌 20a, 20b, 27, 27b, 42, 42c, 123;
🚉 Clontarf Rd

You won't exactly be cashing in
your chips at this casino, which
literally means small house.
Roman temple from the outside
and kooky Georgian house inside,
it is one of Ireland's finest – and
weirdest – Palladian buildings.
The house was built by Sir William Chambers for the eccentric
James Caulfield (1728–99). While
externally the building appears
to contain just the one room, the
interior is a convoluted maze of
rooms.

GAA MUSEUM

☎ 819 2323; http://museum.gaa.ie;
St Joseph's Ave, Croke Park; general
admission admission €5.50/4/15,
museum & stadium tour €9.50/7/24;
⏰ 9.30am-5pm Mon-Sat (to 6pm Jul &
Aug), from noon Sun (New Stand ticket
holders only on match days); 🚌 3, 11,
11a, 16, 16a, 123; 🚉 Connolly Station;
♿ excellent

Sporting enthusiasts will
absolutely love this museum at
the state-of-the-art Croke Park

WORTH THE TRIP: CLONTARF

Just 4.6km northeast of the centre,
Clontarf is a pretty bayside suburb
whose main attractions are birds and
golf. The **North Bull Wall**, which extends about 1km into Dublin Bay, was
built in 1820 to stop Dublin Harbour
from silting up. Marshes and dunes
developed behind the wall, creating
North Bull Island which is now a
Unesco biosphere reserve. The bird
population can reach 40,000 – watch
for shelducks, curlews and oystercatch-
ers on the mud flats – and a range of
plants and other animals can be seen.
An **interpretive centre** (☎ 833
8341; admission free; ⏰ times vary,
call ahead) on the island is reached by
walking across the 1.5km-long northern causeway. Transport to the island
is poor. Catch the DART to Raheny,
from where it's a 40-minute walk to
the northern causeway, or catch bus
130 from Lower Abbey St to the Bull
Wall stop, within a 25-minute walk.

---

stadium, which explores the
history of hurling, Gaelic football,
camogie (women's variant of
hurling) and handball, from their
ancient roots to the present day.
Interactive screens let you test
your skills, listen to recordings
from special matches and replay
historic moments. You can also
tour the grounds and dressing
rooms with a guide.

NEIGHBOURHOODS

BEYOND THE ROYAL CANAL

ⓒ NATIONAL BOTANIC GARDENS

☎ 837 4388; Glasnevin, enter from Botanic Ave; admission free; ⊙ 9am-6pm Apr-Oct, 10am-4.30pm Nov-Mar; 🚍 13, 19, 83; ♿ excellent

Recharge your batteries among meandering arboretum trails, river Dodder walks and Victorian rose gardens. An important centre of horticultural and botanical study for more than 200 years, there are more than 20,000 plant varieties spread over the garden's almost 20 hectares.

ⓒ PROSPECT CEMETERY

☎ 830 1133; www.glasnevin-cemetery .ie; Glasnevin, enter from Finglas Rd; admission free; ⊙ 8am-5pm Mon-Sat, free garden tours from visitor centre 2.30pm Sun; 🚍 40, 40a; ♿ good

Prospect is Ireland's largest Catholic cemetery. It was established in 1832 and is a setting for part of *Ulysses*. A walk along its quiet pebbled paths among the huge yew trees and gothic tombs decorated with black wrought-iron railings is about as creepy as it gets in daylight. Many of the monuments are overtly patriotic,

WORTH THE TRIP: HOWTH & MALAHIDE

Two lovely seaside villages sit on Dublin Bay's northern end. **Howth** (rhymes with 'both'), 15km northeast of central Dublin and accessible by DART, has a pleasant port with three piers, some good pubs and excellent fish and chip joints. Looming above it is the **Hill of Howth**, wonderful for a leisurely half- or full-day's walk with views of Dublin city and the bay.

About 1.5km offshore is **Ireland's Eye**, a rocky seabird sanctuary with the ruins of a 6th-century monastery. There's a Martello tower at the island's northwestern end, while at the eastern end a spectacular rock face plummets into the sea. Seals can also be spotted. **Doyle & Sons** (☎ 831 4200) runs boats out to the island from the East Pier of Howth Harbour during summer from around 10.30am on weekends. Return trips cost €10.

Malahide's main attraction is **Malahide Castle** (☎ 846 2184; admission €6.70/5.70), set in 1 sq km of parklands. The castle served as the Talbot family home from 1185 to 1976 and incorporates a hotchpotch of architectural styles from the 12th to the 18th centuries. On the grounds is the **Fry Model Railway** and **Tara's Palace** (☎ 846 3779; admission by donation; ⊙ 10.45am-4.45pm Mon-Sat, 11.30am-5.30pm Sun Apr-Sep), an elaborate, oversized doll's house whose rooms are furnished with fittings from around the world. The **Talbot Botanic Gardens** (☎ 872 7777; admission €4; ⊙ 2-5pm May-Sep), also within the estate's grounds, has a varied collection of plants, many from the southern hemisphere. Catch bus 42 from Busáras or the DART from Connolly Station.

National Botanic Gardens

adorned with national symbols. Others are poignantly customised with sporting paraphernalia or old toys. The watchtowers in the walls were used to watch for body snatchers working for the city's 19th-century surgeons. Steady your nerves afterwards in one of Dublin's most authentic traditional pubs, Kavanagh's, or the Gravediggers as it's known, at Prospect Sq.

⭐ PLAY

⭐ HELIX

☎ 700 7000; www.thehelix.ie; Cons Ave, Glasnevin; 🚌 4, 11, 13, 19; ♿ excellent; 🎭 special shows

The northside's beautifully designed arts centre at Dublin City University has three venues hosting a range of shows, from music and theatre to ballet and opera. Dame Kiri Te Kanawa and Lou Reed have graced its floorboards.

⭐ NATIONAL AQUATIC CENTRE

☎ 646 4300; www.nac.ie; Snugborough Rd, Blanchardstown; admission €12/10; 🕙 11am-10pm Mon-Fri, 9am-8pm Sat & Sun; 🚌 38a from Hawkins St

Established in 2003 to accommodate the Special Olympics World Summer Games, this is the largest indoor water park in Europe. Besides its Olympic-size competition pool it has fantastic water roller coasters, wave and surf machines, a leisure pool and all types of flumes. Be prepared to join the shivering line of children queuing for slides on weekend afternoons.

Tripod (p96)

DRINKING

The pub is as much a part of the essential experience of visiting Dublin as being the victim of rudeness in Paris or being bumped on the busy sidewalks of New York. Go on, admit it: chances are you've come to sample the mythical atmosphere of a proper Dublin pub – the raucous conversations, the philosophical observations that only make sense after a couple of drinks, the joke-telling competitions, the impromptu and often atonal sing-songs…and the beer: the pints of black velvet beauty adorned with the Guinness harp. For no matter how sophisticated and cosmopolitan Dublin has become, the pub remains the alpha and omega of all Dublin social life. You will *never* understand this city or its people if you don't cross the pub's welcoming threshold and settle in for a night whose outcome you shouldn't even try to predict.

There are pubs for every taste and sensibility, although the traditional haunt populated by flat-capped pensioners bursting with insightful anecdotes is disappearing under a modern wave of designer bars and themed locales that wouldn't seem out of place in any other big city.

Many are packed to the rafters most nights, particularly around touristy Temple Bar, which often feels like Ibiza in the rain. There are many busy, sociable and traditional bars on either side of Grafton St. Wexford/Camden St in SoDa is the new corridor of cool, although Dawson St, which it replaced, is still putting up a fight, while the quays, for so long the poster-child for grim old Dublin, have some terrific spots worth checking out. Georgian Dublin has a good mix of pubs, most of which fill up with office workers after hours (although that's not as unattractive a proposition as it might sound elsewhere).

From Monday to Thursday pubs stop serving at 11.30pm, on Friday and Saturday it's 12.30am, and Sunday 11pm, with half an hour's drink-up time each night. Several city-centre bars have late licences. For the latest on the city's pubs, check out www.dublinpubs.ie.

TOP FIVE PUBS FOR...
- > A decent pint and a chat – Grogan's Castle Lounge (p94)
- > Beats and beatniks – Anseo (p92)
- > Fiddles and bodhráns – Palace Bar (p77)
- > Getting jiggy wid it – Village (p97)
- > The perfect Cosmo – Octagon Bar (p76)

TOP DJ BARS
- > Anseo (p92)
- > Bia Bar (p92)
- > Village (p97)

DUBLIN'S LANDMARK PUBS
- > Oldest – Brazen Head (p107)
- > Smallest – Dawson Lounge (Map p39, B5)
- > Longest – Long Hall (p95)

GOING SOLO
- > Globe (p94)
- > Grogan's Castle Lounge (p94)
- > Kehoe's (p50)
- > Solas (p95)
- > Mulligans (p76)

Opposite Members of the SBC – the Sad Bastard's Corner at the Cobblestone (p126)

KIDS

Dublin is a reasonably child-friendly city but it does have its drawbacks.
The main problem is infrastructure – poor transport means lots of walking, there are few public spots to stop and rest (particularly on the northside), and trendification means many pubs are not as family-friendly as
they used to be. Bear in mind that under-16s are banned from pubs after
7pm – even if they're accompanied by their parents – but the plus side
is that under-fives travel free on all public transport and most admission
prices have an under-16s reduced fee.

There's also a dearth of public toilets in the city centre, although the major shopping centres have toilets and baby-change facilities. Although breast-feeding in Dublin is not an especially common sight (Ireland has one of the lowest rates of it in the world), you can do so with impunity pretty much anywhere and you won't get so much as a stare.

A good number of restaurants accept child diners, though it's best to arrive early in the evening. Many hotels in Dublin provide babysitting services (normally €9 to €10 per hour) or, though more expensive, you could try a couple of agencies who provide professional nannies. It's up to you to negotiate a fee with the nanny but €10 or €11 per hour is the average, plus taxi fare. Agencies include **Belgrave Agency** (☎ 280 9341; 55 Mulgrave St, Dun Laoghaire; per hr €15 plus 21% VAT), **Executive Nannies** (☎ 873 1273; 43 Lower Dominick St; per hr €15-20) and **Babysitters Ireland** (www.babysitters.ie; 7a Sweetman Ave, Blackrock; per hr €8-10).

Practicalities aside, the increased wealth of Dubliners has spurned a variety of children's activities; the best of which can be found in the **Ark** (☎ 670 7788; www.ark.ie; 11a Eustace St; admission varies; ⏰ Sat & Sun, activity times vary), a cultural centre for kids; Dvblinia (p99) and, of course, Dublin Zoo (p121). The National Aquatic Centre (p141) is a great spot for kids, as are the Airfield Trust Gardens (p129), especially the vintage cars. Also worth checking out are the weekend or holiday kids' programmes at the National Gallery of Ireland (p57), National Museum (p59), Irish Museum of Modern Art (p102) and Dublin City Gallery – Hugh Lane (p110). The Temple Bar Diversions festival (p25) is also a great option.

TOP SIGHTS FOR KIDS
> Airfield Trust Garden (p129)
> Dvblinia (p99)
> Dublin Zoo (p121)
> Kilmainham Gaol (p103)
> Malahide Castle (p140)

TOP ACTIVITIES
> Making ceramics in the Ark (www.ark.ie)
> National Gallery painting class (p57)
> Splashing about the National Aquatic Centre (p141)
> Viking Splash Tours (p172)

Opposite Brazen Head (p107)

SNAPSHOTS

ARCHITECTURE

With one incredible exception and a handful of new efforts, Dublin doesn't really earn a lot of architectural kudos. Too much urban planning by tasteless, myopic and greedy developers is the usual excuse, and we'll stick to it too. The big exception, of course, is Dublin's Georgian heritage, visible in not just the fine residences and public buildings but the wide roads, gardens and elegant squares that were laid out from roughly 1780 to 1830.

Buildings of note from the 20th century include: Busáras (Map p109, D4), the International Modernist bus station designed by Michael Scott in the 1940s, and Paul Koralek's 1967 Berkeley Library at Trinity (Map p39, C3). The 1990s redevelopment of Temple Bar signalled the start of a major architectural renewal that continues to this day. In recent years, the biggest change in Dublin's landscape has been the development of the docklands, with the arrival of the International Financial Services Centre and huge development of Spencer Dock and the Point Village. Celebrated polish architect Daniel Libeskind is due to unveil the Grand Canal Performing Arts Centre there in 2008 and building is under way on the new 80m U2 Tower at Sir John Rogerson's Quay.

Reflecting City (www.reflectingcity.com) offers virtual tours of all the major urban renewal areas, while **Archèire** (www.irish-architecture.com) is a comprehensive site covering all things to do with Irish architecture and design.

THE BEST OF GEORGIAN
> Custom House (p110)
> Four Courts (p124)
> Leinster House (p57)
> Powerscourt Centre (Map p39, A3)
> Newman House (p59)

BEST BRIDGES
> Ha'penny Bridge (Map p67, C3)
> Grattan Bridge (Map p67, B3)
> James Joyce Bridge
> O'Connell Bridge (Map p109, C5)
> Millennium Bridge (Map p67, B3)

CLUBBING

Not quite the clubbers' paradise that it was for a brief, crazy and e-fuelled moment in the late 1990s, Dublin's clubbing scene tends to huddle around the safe middle ground. Still there's no lack of choice if you want to dance (part of) the night away. The spread of late-night bars advertising loud music and booze without an admission fee have certainly dented the clubs' monopoly on late-night fun, but then again 'late night' is a relative term: party-pooping opening hours – with their 2.30am finishing-up times – will shock all but British visitors. But, misery loves company, and you'll be among tens of thousands as you stumble into the night looking for a ride home.

Everybody seems to flock to Temple Bar, where you'll find a couple of great clubs. If you want to do a little celebrity spotting then hit the clubs around Grafton St, but we think SoDa is your best bet for just good old dancing – from Rí Rá (p96) to the brand-new Tripod (p96) you'll find a handful of clubs to suit your needs, whether it be charty R'n'B or the dirtiest electro beats.

Check out *Mongrel* or the *Event Guide* – both free – for listings, or go online at www.dublinnightclubs.ie.

TOP FIVE CLUBS
> Rí Rá (p96)
> Tripod (p96)
> Rogue (p79)
> Hub (p78)
> Temple Bar Music Centre (p79)

TOP FIVE CLUB NIGHTS
> **Bodytonic** (Wax @ Spy; www .bodytonicmusic.com; ☻ Fri)
> **Firehouse Skank** (Hub; ☻ Sat)
> **Hospital** (Traffic; ☎ 873 4800; 54 Middle Abbey St; ☻ Fri)
> **Pogo** (Tripod; ☻ Sat)
> **Strictly Handbag** (Rí Rá; ☻ Mon)

TOP FIVE CLUBS TO DRESS UP FOR
> Lillies Bordello (p50)
> Renard's (p65)
> **Sin** (☎ 633 4232; Sycamore St, Temple Bar)
> Rí Rá (p96)
> Tripod (p96)

TOP FIVE DJS TO LOOK OUT FOR
> Arveene
> Billy Scurry
> Bodytonic
> Barry Redsetta
> DJ Morgan

FOOD

Good news for foodies visiting Dublin: the market is changing, and for the better. Restaurateurs have finally twigged the idea that not every meal has to be a once-a-year splurge and that wallet-friendly menus mean more bankable turnover. They're happy and we're happy. All over Dublin, thankfully, midpriced restaurants are cropping up that offer very good food at competitive prices.

You can still eat French (and Irish) *haute cuisine* any night of the week but you'll also find Nepalese, Brazilian and pretty much everything in between.

The most concentrated restaurant area is Temple Bar, but apart from a handful of good places, the bulk of eateries offer bland, unimaginative fodder and cheap set menus for tourists. Better food and service can usually be found on either side of Grafton St, while the top-end restaurants are clustered around Merrion Sq and Fitzwilliam Sq. Fast-food chains dominate the northside, though some fine cafés and eateries are finally appearing there too.

Ireland has excellent beef, pork, seafood, dairy foods and winter vegetables, and many good restaurants now source their ingredients locally, from organic and artisan producers.

For many restaurants, particularly those in the centre, it's worth booking for Friday or Saturday nights to ensure a table.

TOP FIVE FOOD FAVES
> Best brunch – Odessa (p92)
> Best ethnic – Monty's of Kathmandu (p75)
> Best informal grub – Gruel (p74)
> Best lunch – L'Gueuleton (p91)
> Best splurge – Thornton's (p48)

TABLES WITH VIEWS
> Thornton's (p48)
> Ocean (p136)
> Winding Stair (p115)
> Enoteca Delle Langhe (p118)

GAELIC FOOTBALL

Hurling and football (not to be confused with Association Football, the *other* game) are the main sports of the **Gaelic Athletic Association** (www.gaa .ie) which have a massive national following. Hurling – a super-fast game played with flat sticks and lots of skill – is the more elegant sport, but in Dublin it's all about football, where a round ball is kicked along the ground soccer-style, or passed between players as in rugby. The game is very popular in the north Dublin suburbs, where most of the county's best clubs are based – but if you want a genuinely enthralling local experience, try to get to **Croke Park** (Map p109, D1; ☎ 836 3222; www.crokepark.ie; Dublin 3; 🚌 3, 11, 11a, 16, 16a, 51a from O'Connell St; 🚉 Connolly Station) to watch the Dublin county team play in either the winter-time National League or the more rewarding All Ireland Championship, which runs roughly from April to the third Sunday in September.

The Dubs – who play in two tones of blue – are a traditional powerhouse of the game, having won the championship 22 times, second only to their great rivals Kerry. Their fans are best described as boisterous: when they're not singing 'Molly Malone' or 'Dublin in the Rare Auld Times' they can be heard letting the opposition know exactly what they think of them.

THE BEST OF THE BOYS IN BLUE

Dublin fans could debate the following list for an eternity:
> Anton O'Toole
> Jimmy Keaveney
> Brian Mullins
> Paul Curran
> Brian Cullen

BEST DUBLIN GAMES IN RECENT MEMORY
> Dublin vs Meath, 1991
> Dublin vs Mayo, 2006
> Dublin vs Kerry, 1978
> Dublin vs Donegal, 1992
> Dublin vs Kerry, 1977

GARDENS & PARKS

Not only does Dublin have a handful of the most beautifully manicured Georgian parks in Europe, but it is also home to the world's largest – wait for it – enclosed, nonwildlife, city park in the world. Despite the qualifiers, Phoenix Park (p125) – all 709 magnificent hectares of it – is larger than *all* of the major London parks…put together. Fallow deer, a zoo, sports grounds aplenty, the president's gaff, what more could one want?

Not nearly as big but impressive for a host of other reasons are Dublin's Georgian squares. St Stephen's Green (p61) is the city's most frequented – on a summer's day you can barely find a spot of green to lay your head on, for the numbers sprawled out on its beautifully kept lawns. Merrion Sq (p57) is probably more gorgeous still, Fitzwilliam Sq (p53) is small but perfectly proportioned, but our favourite spot of all are the relatively unknown Iveagh Gardens (p53), a stone's throw from St Stephen's Green but miles away in tranquillity and peace.

The northside city centre is a little devoid of green space. Even the once lovely Mountjoy Sq, laid out when the area was the favourite domicile of the Anglo-Irish gentry, has lost much of its green appeal.

TOP FIVE GREEN ACTIVITIES

> A cricket match at Phoenix Cricket Club in Phoenix Park
> Feeding the ducks at St Stephen's Green
> A lunchtime summer's gig at the bandstand, St Stephen's Green
> Reading the witty commentary on the Oscar Wilde Statue, Merrion Sq
> Polo – the one with horses – in Phoenix Park

TOP FIVE SPOTS FOR A ROMANTIC LIAISON

> The rocks in St Stephen's Green
> The secluded middle of Merrion Sq
> At the back of the Iveagh Gardens
> By the polo grounds in Phoenix Park – but in the daytime only!
> Anywhere in Fitzwilliam Sq

GAY & LESBIAN

Dublin's not a bad place to be gay. Most people wouldn't bat an eyelid at public displays of affection between same-sex couples, or cross-dressing in the city centre, but discretion is advised in the suburbs. If you are harassed on the streets don't hesitate to call the **Gay & Lesbian Garda Liaison Officer** (☎ 666 9000) or the **Sexual Assault Unit** (☎ 666 000, Pearse St Garda Station).

There is a range of useful organisations, publications and online resources.

Gay Men's Health Project (☎ 660 2189) Practical advice on men's health issues.

Gay Switchboard Dublin (☎ 872 1055; www.gayswitchboard.ie; ☽ 7.30am-9.30pm Mon-Fri, 3.30-6pm Sat) A friendly and useful voluntary service that can advise on everything from finding accommodation to legal issues.

Lesbian Line (☎ 872 9911; ☽ 7-9pm Thu)

National Lesbian & Gay Federation (NLGF; ☎ 01-671 9076; 2 Scarlett Row, Temple Bar) Publishes *Gay Community News* (www.gcn.ie), a free news- and issues-based monthly paper.

Outhouse (☎ 873 4932; www.outhouse.ie; 105 Capel St) Gay, lesbian and bisexual resource centre. Great stop-off point to see what's on, check noticeboards and meet people. It publishes the free Ireland's *Pink Pages*, a directory of gay-centric services which is also accessible on the website.

Most of the city's hotels wouldn't bat an eyelid if same-sex couples checked in, but the same can't be said of many of the city's B&Bs. However there are a couple of exclusively gay B&Bs.

Frankies Guesthouse (☎ 478 3087; www.frankiesguesthouse.com; 8 Camden Pl) Twelve homey rooms in an old mews house, with cable TV, full Irish breakfast and a plant-filled roof terrace.

Inn on the Liffey (☎ 677 0828; innontheliffey@hotmail.com; 21 Upper Ormond Quay) Compact no-frills rooms on the northside quays, and guests have free access to the Dock sauna.

TOP GAY CLUB NIGHTS

> **Casting Couch** (Front Lounge, 33 Parliament St, Temple Bar; ☽ Tue)
> **Kiss** (Temple Bar Music Centre, p77; ☽ Fri)
> **Space 'N' Veda** (The George, S Great George's St, SoDa; ☽ Wed)
> **Strictly Handbag** (Rí Rá, p96; ☽ Mon)

TOP FIVE GAY NIGHTS…THAT AREN'T A CLUB

> **Bingo** (Front Lounge, 33 Parliament St, Temple Bar; ☽ Sun)
> **Hanki Panki** (Rogue, p79; ☽ Tue)
> **DJ Lounge** (GUBU, p119; ☽ Sat)
> **VIQ** (Sin, 17-19 Sycamore St, Temple Bar; ☽ Mon)
> **Ivanna's Quiz Night** (GUBU, p119; ☽ 1st Mon of month)

SNAPSHOTS

JAMES JOYCE

One of the most over-quoted stories regarding Joyce relates to his boast that if Dublin were ever flattened by an earthquake or some other disaster, the city could be rebuilt down to the last stone by following the descriptions in *Ulysses,* such was his painstaking and accurate portrayal of his home town. Times – and the city – have moved on since then, and while Joyce remains very much in the foreground of Dublin's rich literary heritage, his appeal to the modern Dubliner has been coated in a layer of dust that is only ever blown off by those with a keen interest in great books and visitors on an intellectual nostalgia buzz. Still, Joyce was a genius, and he was Dublin's genius, so the tourist office make a big deal of Bloomsday and any other Joyce-related tidbits.

On 16 June each year, Joyce-lovers take to the streets in a re-enactment of Leopold Bloom's journey around Dublin in *Ulysses*. You can don Edwardian gear and join in on the Bloomsday fun (see www.jamesjoyce.ie). Various readings and dramatisations from Joyce's works take place around the city as folk in period costume, c 1904, chow down on Gorgonzola cheese and glasses of Burgundy. Points of activity include the James Joyce Museum at Sandycove (p133), where *Ulysses* begins, Sweny's Chemist, Davy Byrne's pub (Map p39, B4) and the National Library (p57).

At other times of the year you can visit the sites most associated with the writer (see boxed text below), or you can try to read *Ulysses*. We recommend that you read *Dubliners,* for our money still the best book written by anyone born within the canal boundaries.

TOP FIVE JOYCE LANDMARKS
> James Joyce House of the Dead (p103)
> Leopold & Molly Bloom's House (Map p109, A2)
> James Joyce Centre (p112)
> Newman House (p59)
> James Joyce Museum (p133)

TOP FIVE JOYCE QUOTES
> A man's errors are his portals of discovery.

> Christopher Columbus, as every one knows, is honoured by posterity because he was the last to discover America.
> Irresponsibility is part of the pleasure of all art; it is the part the schools cannot recognise.
> There is no heresy or no philosophy which is so abhorrent to the church as a human being.
> Come forth, Lazarus! And he came fifth and lost the job.

LIVE MUSIC

Dublin may be small, but it rocks. Virtually every decent pop and rock act in the world has added Dublin to its touring schedule, and they're rewarded with big, enthusiastic crowds who are renowned for cheering their favourite artists, raising the energy levels to an almost unbelievable degree. Just ask Garth Brooks, or Robbie Williams, both of whom have stated publicly that playing Dublin was one of the highlights of their career. (We prefer to name-check Guns 'n' Roses, who also loved the city, but hey, different strokes…)

There are venues of all sizes – including Phoenix Park (Map p122-3, A4), which hosts crowds of up to 135,000 – but the best gigs are generally in midsized venues where the atmosphere can get really turbo-charged. Intimate Whelans (p97) is the home of the balladeers and singer-song-writers, while next door the Village (p97) plays host to a motley crew of performers, from hip-hop to thrash metal. If you're veering towards the rootsy side of things, Vicar Street (p107) in the Liberties hosts a fabulous range of acts, from African folk bands to the great names of American soul. Finally, the wonderful Olympia Theatre (p79) has seen some of the best gigs, including the likes of Wolf Mother and Radiohead.

TOP FIVE ALBUMS…
> *The Unforgettable Fire*, U2
> *Music in Mouth*, Bell X1
> *In Towers & Clouds*, The Immediate
> *The Fine Art of Resurfacing*,
  Boomtown Rats
> *Live & Dangerous*, Thin Lizzy

TOP FIVE DUBLIN SONGS
> *Raglan Road*, Luke Kelly & The Dubliners
> *Lay Me Down*, The Frames
> *One*, U2
> *Still in Love with You*, Thin Lizzy
> *I Don't Like Mondays*, Boomtown Rats

SHOPPING

Dubliners might be fairly new to the shopping-as-pastime craze, but they've taken to it with a gusto normally reserved for a pub's last-drinks call. On weekends, shopping districts are chock-a-block with teenagers, families, tourists and the odd elderly lady bravely making her way through the chaos. Unless you enjoy the hustle and bustle, save your shopping for weekdays – the earlier the better.

British and US chains dominate, but there are numerous independent shops selling high-quality, locally made goods. Irish designer clothing, handmade jewellery, unusual homewares and crafts, and cheeses to die for are readily available if you know where to look. While souvenir hunters can still buy Guinness magnets and shamrock tea towels, a new breed of craft shop offers one-off or limited-edition souvenirs. Traditional Irish products, such as crystal and knitwear, remain popular and you can find modern takes on the classics. Most shops are open from 9am or 10am to 6pm Monday to Saturday (until 8pm Thursday) and from noon to 6pm Sunday. Almost all accept credit cards, and ATMs are everywhere.

Try the following hot shopping spots for starters:

Grafton St (Map p39, B4) Boutiques, department stores, clothing and music chains.
West of Grafton St (Map p39, A4) Small, funky independent clothing and jewellery shops.
East of Grafton St (Map p39, B4) Antiques and traditional crafts, art galleries.
Temple Bar (Map p67, C3) Record shops, vintage clothes, kooky knick-knacks, markets.
Henry St (Map p109, B4) High-street chains, department stores, sportswear.
Talbot St Map p109, D4) Bargain-basement clothes, homewares, furnishings and hardware.
Capel St (Map p109, A5) Outdoor gear, car accessories, cheap furniture, sex toys.
Francis St (Map pp100-1, H3) Antiques.

TOP FIVE GUARANTEED IRISH
> Avoca Handweavers (p42)
> Barry Doyle Design Jewellers (p84)
> Cathach Books (p42)
> Louis Copeland (p114)
> Weir & Sons (p46)

TOP FIVE MUSEUM SHOPS
> Chester Beatty Library (p82)
> Dublin Writers Museum (p111)
> Irish Museum of Modern Art (p102)
> National Gallery of Ireland (p57)
> Trinity College Library Shop (p40)

TOP FIVE BOUTIQUES
> Chica (p42)
> Alias Tom (p41)
> 5 Scarlet Row (p69)
> Smock (p71)
> Costume (p84)

TRADITIONAL MUSIC

Dublin has always had an ambivalent relationship with traditional music. Many middle-class Dubliners, eager to bask in a more 'cosmopolitan' light, have been largely dismissive of the genre as belonging to less progressive rural types with nicotine-coloured fingers and beer-stained beards. Instead, they packed their CD collections with 'world music' – folk and traditional music from *other* cultures. In the last few years, however, the irony has become all-too apparent and there has been a slow (and often grudging) recognition that one of the richest and most evocative veins of traditional expression is on their very doorstep.

Consequently, you'll find a number of pubs that put on scheduled and improvised 'sessions' attended for the most part by foreign visitors who frankly appreciate the form far more than most Dubs and will relish any opportunity to drink and toe-tap to some extraordinary virtuoso performances.

Comhaltas Ceoltó iri Éireann (p136) is the spiritual headquarters of the traditional forms in Dublin – the Friday night *céilidh* (group Irish dance) is one of the highlights of any visit to the city. Smithfield is home to two of the best traditional bars in the city, the Cobblestone (p126) and Hughes' Bar (p126) – if you're looking for that old-fashioned atmosphere these are the places to go. Otherwise, check out our list below.

Want to take some music home? Pay a visit to Claddagh Records (p70) where you'll find a massive collection and a friendly, knowledgeable staff who will help you discern between jigs and reels, *bodhráns* (Irish drums) and bouzoukis.

TOP FIVE TRADITIONAL SESSIONS
> **Cobblestone** (p126; 🕑 nightly) Best on a Thursday.
> **Devitt's** (p96; 🕑 9.30pm Thu-Sat)
> **Ha'penny Bridge Inn** (p77; 🕑 9-11pm Fri)
> **Hughes' Bar** (p126; 🕑 from 9pm nightly)
> **Palace Bar** (p77; 🕑 from 8.30pm Tue, Wed & Sun)

TOP FIVE TRADITIONAL MUSICIANS
> The Chieftains
> Bothy Band
> Tommy Peoples
> Andy Irvine
> Paddy Keenan

THEATRE

Dubliners have a unique affinity with theatre; it seems to course through their veins. Perhaps this explains why dramatists Oliver Goldsmith, Oscar Wilde and George Bernard Shaw conquered the theatre world in London even before there was such an entity as Irish drama. While Dublin has a long association with the stage – the first theatre was founded here in 1637 – it wasn't until the late-19th-century Celtic Revival Movement and the establishment of the Abbey Theatre (p118) that Irish drama really took off.

After years in the doldrums following the successes of famous playwrights Wilde, Yeats, Shaw and Beckett, Irish theatre is undergoing something of a renaissance. The Abbey has found a couple of new stars in Conor McPherson and Mark O'Rowe, while the Gate (p119) does a roaring trade in high-quality productions usually starring a big name or two – don't be surprised to see a big-time Hollywood star treading these particular boards.

If you want something different, and there are a number of new companies staging thought-provoking, contemporary plays, you'll have to settle for smaller venues and spaces, including converted pub rooms. Look out for the likes of **Rough Magic** (www.rough-magic.com).

Theatre bookings can usually be made by quoting a credit-card number over the phone; you can collect your tickets just before the performance. Expect to pay anything between €12 and €20 for most shows, with some costing as much as €25. Most plays begin between 8pm and 8.30pm. Check out www.irishtheatreonline.com.

Malahide Castle (p140)

BACKGROUND

HISTORY

ORIGINS

A casual walk around the city centre doesn't reveal much of Dublin's history from before the middle of the 18th century. Besides the city's modern Irish name, Baile Átha Claith, meaning 'Town of the Hurdle Ford' – in reference to the original Celtic settlement on the Liffey's northern bank – there is absolutely no visible evidence that the Iron Age Celts ever arrived here. But they did, around 700 BC.

Even the three 12th-century behemoths of the Norman occupation – Dublin Castle, and Christchurch and St Patrick's Cathedrals – which ushered in 800 years of British rule, owe more to Victorian home improvements than they do their original fittings. The famous well by the side of St Patrick's, where the saint is said to have baptised the heathen Irish into Christianity in the 5th century, is nothing more than a story told to visitors.

GEORGIAN DUBLIN

To get a tangible sense of Dublin's history, fast-forward through the occupation, past the outbreaks of plague and the introduction of the Penal Laws prohibiting Catholics from owning or being much of anything, until the middle of the 18th century. It was then that the Protestant gentry decided that the squalid medieval burg they lived in wasn't quite the gleaming metropolis they deserved, and set about redesigning the whole place, to create Georgian Dublin.

Scarcely had the scaffolding come down on the refurbishments, however, when the Act of Union in 1801 caused Dublin to lose its 'second city of the Empire' appeal and descend into a kind of ghost-town squalor.

DISASTER & INDEPENDENCE

While Dublin escaped the worst effects of the Potato Famine (1845–51), when the staple crop was blighted by disease leading to the death of

---

DUBLIN'S PALE

The phrase 'beyond the pale' originated when Anglo-Norman control over Ireland was restricted to the narrow eastern coastal strip surrounding Dublin, known as the Pale. Outside this area – or 'Beyond the Pale' – Ireland remained a wild place, and fierce Irish warriors launched regular raids on English forces from their strongholds in the Wicklow mountains.

---

at least one million, the forced emigration of another million or so and the general collapse of Irish rural society, Dublin's streets and squares became flooded with starving rural refugees. The British government's refusal to really address the gravity of the situation fuelled rebellious instincts; while the 19th century is littered with glorious but vain attempts to strike a blow at British power, after the Famine it was only a matter of time. Following another ill-planned revolt at Easter 1916 – which laid waste to much of the city centre and resulted in the leaders' execution in the grounds of Kilmainham Gaol – the tide turned firmly in favour of full-blown independence, which was achieved after a war of sorts lasting from 1920 to '21.

FROM FREE STATE TO CELTIC TIGER

The partition of Ireland that followed the War of Independence wasn't to everyone's liking, so a Civil War quickly ensued – more bloody and savage than the war against British rule. Thereafter, Ireland settled cautiously into its new-found freedom: conservative and Catholic, it moved carefully through the 20th century until the 1960s, when the first winds of liberal thinking began to blow. Universal free secondary education was introduced and the Republic joined the European Economic Community in 1973.

Dublin's economic climate changed dramatically in the 1990s as interest rates tumbled, business burgeoned and (mostly US) foreign investment injected capital and led to hugely reduced unemployment. The now legendary Celtic Tiger economy continued unabated for 10 years. A mini post-Millennium lull quickly passed, with spending rising to an all-time high. Economists are sounding alarm bells though. The housing industry is stretched to meet demand, and climbing interest rates and

---

DIVIDED WE FALL

Dublin is split, physically and psychologically, by the River Liffey. Traditionally, areas north of the river have been poorer and more rundown, while the south boasts well-kept squares, expensive shops, restaurants and bars. But some Dubliners insist the real divide is east–west, with the wealthiest suburbs nearest the bay and the poorest suburbs to the west.

The 1960s and '70s saw major urban renewal and whole communities, who had spent generations in the inner city, uprooted and rehoused in new towns such as Ballymun and Darndale. The lucrative land was then rezoned for commercial use, but some say the heart and soul of the city was broken.

---

inflation in 2006, as well as punitively high wage costs are steering many companies to cheaper markets in Eastern Europe and Asia.

LIFE AS A DUBLINER

More than 50% of Dubliners are under 28 and almost a quarter are under 15 – a fact which goes a long way to explaining the city's vibrant, liberal outlook. They are, by and large, a relaxed and easy-going bunch, generally more at home with informality than any kind of stuffiness. Which isn't to say that there aren't a few upturned noses about town – a massive injection of prosperity will almost guarantee it – but years of British rule fostered a healthy contempt for snobbery and it is generally money, rather than breeding, which impresses here.

The population of greater Dublin is almost 1.6 million. Although the city is predominantly white and Roman Catholic, the substantial Protestant and Muslim minorities have been joined in recent years by immigrants from Africa and Eastern Europe.

Their assimilation into a city that hitherto knew only its own is nothing short of remarkable, although it'll be some years yet before the two-way stream of cultural influence is really flowing; before the presence of Akara pancakes on a restaurant menu is met with no surprise; or locals become adept at telling the difference between eight kinds of Polish vodkas. Unfortunately, however, the rapid growth in immigration has also exposed the raw nerves of racism in the city, with attacks and abuse all too common.

Probably the strictest set of social rules apply to the pub, and specifically to the buying of drinks. The rounds system – whereby you take it in

DID YOU KNOW?

> Some 12% of workers travel more than 30km to work each day, more than double the distance in 1981
> If the whole of Ireland had a population density of Dublin it would have more than 300 million people
> The average industrial weekly wage is €609 for men and €430 for women
> Around 9800 pints of beer are drunk each hour by Dubliners from Friday night to Monday morning
> The average price for a house is €430,000
> Women outnumber men in Dublin by 20,000

turns to buy a drink for everyone in your group – is integral to pub life, and nothing says 'social pariah' faster than disrupting the balance: farting in church will a least earn you a few laughs.

Which leads us neatly to religion. Younger Dubliners aren't especially religious, and the notion of sex, religion and politics being taboo subjects for discussion seems to have gone by the wayside; most young Dubs are disenchanted with religion and politics, but sex will always garner a willing audience!

Nonsmokers will have a field day in Dublin, as the smoking ban instituted in 2004 has been remarkably successful. Ironically, many of the outdoor smoking areas of bars and clubs have become the place to hang and local magazines have been rating best smoking areas for action, pick-ups and romance.

GOVERNMENT & POLITICS

At local level, Dublin is governed by three elected bodies: Dublin City Council supervises the city; a county council looks after Dublin County; and Dun Laoghaire & Rathdown Corporation administers the port town. The city version used to be known as Dublin Corporation (the Corpo), a name synonymous with inefficiency and incompetence, but the new incarnation is a progressive and admired local government. Each year, it elects a Lord Mayor who shifts into the Mansion House, speaks out on matters to do with the city and is lucky if half of Dublin knows his or her name by the time they have to hand back the chains.

ENVIRONMENT

Though Dublin does not suffer the severe air pollution that chokes some other European cities, it has its share of environmental concerns. Worst among them is traffic congestion, which has slowly but surely made gridlock a near-permanent reality of daylight hours throughout the city. Half-arsed efforts to redirect the flow of traffic through certain routes have seemingly made the problem worse, prompting commentators to stop commentating and just throw their hands up in despair.

It's not all bad news though: the long-awaited port tunnel, aimed at pulling most of the heavy traffic off the Liffey quays, finally opened in late 2006; time will tell if it will alleviate the flow of traffic as intended.

On the positive side, the city is blessed with many parks, gardens and squares. The 2002 plastic bag tax, where consumers are charged £0.15

per bag, has been a phenomenal success in reducing usage by 90% and gathering millions of euros for environmental projects. Although recycling is slowly taking off, it is not yet part of the collective consciousness due in part to the government's lack of serious commitment to the issue. There's limited recyclable litter collection, and bring-centres are far from plentiful.

A real plus has been the hi-tech waste-water treatment centre that opened in 2003, and which has already improved the water quality in Dublin Bay. But Dublin residents are still perplexed as to why their tap water, once as drinkable and as tasty as any sporting a fancy French label, still tastes like a metallic mixture.

FURTHER READING

You'll have obviously polished off Joyce's masterpieces, *Ulysses* and *Finnegans Wake,* before arriving in Dublin, but you could have spared yourself the pain of reading the virtually unreadable and stuck with *Dubliners,* a thoroughly brilliant and readable collection of 15 stories set in the city – to our mind still the best Dublin-based book ever written.

A quick name-check of other past Dublin masters such as Flann O'Brien *(At Swim-Two-Birds* and *The Third Policeman),* JP Donleavy *(The Ginger Man),* Brendan Behan *(The Quare Fellow)* and Eilís Dillon *(The Head of the Family)* brings us squarely into the rich world of contemporary Dublin-based fiction. King of the heap, of course, is Roddy Doyle, several of whose books have been turned into films – *The Commitments, The Snapper, The Van* and *Paddy Clarke, Ha Ha Ha* – but Roddy has gone serious of late, with books such as *The Woman Who Walked into Doors* and its sequel, *Paula Spencer,* dealing with domestic violence and drug abuse.

Dublin's most lauded contemporary writer is John Banville, who finally won the Booker Prize in 2005 with *The Sea,* although we reckon *The Book of Evidence,* a pseudo-fictional account of an actual murder that occurred in the Phoenix Park in the 1980s, is his greatest work. Keith Ridgeway is another interesting writer to look out for; his latest book is *The Parts*.

If you're looking for something lighter, the Ross O'Carroll-Kelly series, the latest of which is *Should Have Got Off at Sydney Parade,* is a hilarious piss-take of the mores of Dublin 4, the wealthy southern suburbs where being pretentious and posh is, like, *toe*-tally normal.

Finally, we can't ignore the massive influence of the doyenne of chick lit writers, Maeve Binchy, who has been churning out one bestseller after another since the early '70s. Her latest work is *Quentins,* which is set around a posh Dublin restaurant and includes a familiar set of characters, usually drawn from the Dublin upper-middle classes, who struggle with the day-to-day questions of life.

FILMS & TELEVISION

There are only a handful of good films set in Dublin. John Boorman's *The General* (1998), about infamous gangster Martin Cahill and starring Brendan Gleeson, is pretty good; his most recent effort, *The Tiger's Tail* (2006), also starring Gleeson, as well as Kim Catrall, is absolutely awful. Lenny Abrahamson's *Adam and Paul* (2004) is a well-made portrayal of two Dublin junkies and their quixotic quest for a fix, while Damien O'Donnell's *Inside I'm Dancing* (2004) is a terrific piece about friendship and physical disability.

Neil Jordan's historical epic *Michael Collins* (1996) is mostly set in Dublin; the sets were far more spectacular than some of the accents of the cast – Julia Roberts will never really pass as an Irish colleen. Although the excellent *In the Name of the Father* (1991) is about the Troubles, Jim Sheridan filmed the jail scenes in Kilmainham Gaol.

Gangsters are a favourite theme of Dublin film-makers. Besides the above-mentioned *The General,* Paddy Breathnach's *I Went Down* (1997) – called the Irish Pulp Fiction – and John Crowley's *Intermission* (2004) received a lot of press attention.

As far as TV goes, there have been a bunch of made-for-TV dramas based on the capital city, but the only perpetually running programme is the RTE soap *Fair City,* set in the fictional suburb of Carrigstown. Every conceivable theme is dealt with here, from alcoholism to spousal abuse, from immigration to unemployment. It is RTE's most popular programme, but it is still referred to by some as Fairly Shitty.

TOP FIVE FILMS

> *My Left Foot* (1989; Jim Sheridan)
> *The Dead* (1987; John Huston)
> *The Snapper* (1993; Stephen Frears)
> *Inside I'm Dancing* (2004; Damien O'Donnell)
> *A Man of No Importance* (1994; Suri Krishnamma)

DIRECTORY
TRANSPORT
ARRIVAL & DEPARTURE
AIR

Dublin airport (www.dublin-airport.com) is located 13km north of the city centre.

The airport has a range of facilities including an exchange bureau, post office, a Dublin Tourism office, shops, restaurants, ATMs and pubs.

BOAT

From the UK, **Stena Line** (☎ UK 0990 707 070, Dun Laoghaire 204 7600; www .stenaline.co.uk) has a 1½-hour passenger-and-car service from Holyhead to Dun Laoghaire (☎ 280 1905) and a car-only ferry from Holyhead to **Dublin city ferry terminal** (☎ 855 2222) that takes 3½ hours. **Irish Ferries** (☎ UK 0990 171 717, Dublin 1890 313 131; www.irishferries.com; 2-4 Merrion Row) has ferries from Holyhead to Dublin.

Travel from the Airport

	Taxi	Airlink Express	Aircoach	Bus
Pick-up point	Outside arrivals floor	Outside arrivals floor	Outside arrivals floor	Outside arrivals floor
Drop-off point	Anywhere	No 747: to Busáras (Map p109, D4) & Dublin Bus Office; No 748: to Heuston Station & Connolly Station	15 locations in Dublin: Gresham Hotel, corner of Trinity College & Grafton St, Merrion Sq, Leeson St & Dawson St. Another goes to the International Financial Services Centre & Connolly Station before going north to Malahide	Eden Quay, near O'Connell St
Duration	To centre, 30min (50min in rush hour)	30-40min	30-120min (depending on destination & traffic)	60-90min
Cost	To centre, €20	€5	€7/12	€1.70
Other	Supplementary charge of €1 for airport pick-up & additional charges for baggage	Runs every 10-20 min 5.45am-11.30pm	Runs every 15min 5am-11.30pm (hourly midnight-4am)	Runs every 20min from 5.30am-11.30pm
Contact		☎ 872 0000; www.dublinbus.ie	☎ 844 7118; www.aircoach.ie	☎ 872 0000; www.dublinbus.ie

GETTING AROUND

Dublin's buses and train service do little to ease the appalling street congestion. Getting around the centre is best done on foot or bicycle and trips further out should be timed to avoid rush hours. The LUAS light-rail service is efficient but limited in its coverage.

In this book the Dublin Area Rapid Train (DART)/bus/light rail-stations are noted after the 🚃 / 🚌 / 🚋 symbol in each listing.

TRAVEL PASSES

Excellent-value Rambler bus passes are available for one/three/five/seven days for €5/10.50/16.50/20.

Rail-only passes, for DART and suburban trains, cost €22.50/83 for a week/month. An adult rail-and-bus pass costs €16.70/29.20 for use on three/seven consecutive days (photo ID required).

Bus passes should be bought in advance from Dublin Bus (right)

or from the many ticket agents around the city (look for signs in shop windows). You can buy rail passes from any DART or suburban train station.

BUS

Dublin Bus (☎ 873 4222; www.dublinbus .ie; Upper 59 O'Connell St; 🕑 9am-5.30pm Mon-Fri, to 2pm Sat) has buses that are usually blue and cream double-deckers or small, red and yellow ones called 'Imps'. They run from 6am to 11.30pm, less frequently on Sundays. Fares are calculated on stages travelled, from €0.95 for up to three stages to €1.80 for up to 23. Tender exact change when boarding; if you pay too much a receipt is issued, which is reimbursed at the Dublin Bus office.

Dublin Bus also runs Nitelink buses on 22 routes at 12.30am and 2am Monday to Saturday, with extra services every 20 minutes from 12.30am to 4.30am on Friday and Saturday. Buses depart from

---

ALTERNATE ARRIVAL PLANS

Although the vast majority of visitors will enter and exit Dublin's fair city via the airport, you can do your bit for the environment and arrive by boat – and have a bit of an adventure along the way. From Britain it's a cinch: you can buy a combined train-and-ferry ticket for a fraction of what you'll pay in airfare (yes, even in these budget airline times) or, if you're really on a budget, get a bus-and-ferry ticket – from London it won't cost you more than the price of a meal.

You can also arrive at another Irish port. Rosslare in County Wexford has ferry services from France and southwestern Britain while Larne, a short hop outside Belfast, is served from Stranraer in Scotland. Not only will you get to Dublin easily enough, but you can do some exploring on the way.

Recommended Modes of Transport

	Around Grafton St	Georgian Dublin	Temple Bar	SoDa
Around Grafton St	n/a	Walk 5min	Walk 5min	Walk 5min
Georgian Dublin	Walk 5min	n/a	Walk 10min	Walk 10min
Temple Bar	Walk 5min	Walk 10min	n/a	Walk 10min
SoDa	Walk 5min	Walk 10min	Walk 10min	n/a
Kilmainham & the Liberties	Bus 10min	Bus 15min	Walk 15-30min	Walk 15-30min
O'Connell St	Walk 10min	Walk 15min	Walk 10min	Walk 15min
Smithfield	Walk 15min	Bus 15min	Walk 10min	Walk 20min
Phoenix Park	Bus 20min	Bus 20min	Bus 20min	Bus 25min

around College St, Westmoreland St and D'Olier St (Map p39, B1). Journeys cost about €4.50.

TRAIN
Dublin Area Rapid Transport (DART) runs along the coast as far north as Howth and Malahide and as far south as Bray. Services depart every 10 to 20 minutes, from 6.30am to midnight, and less frequently on Sunday.

One-way tickets from central Dublin to Dun Laoghaire/Howth cost €1.95; to Bray it's €2.80. A one-day unlimited DART ticket costs €7.

LIGHT RAIL
Dublin's new **light-rail system** (LUAS; ☎ 1800 300 604; www.luas.ie) runs one line from Sandyford north to St Stephen's Green and one line from Tallaght east via Heuston Station

---

CLIMATE CHANGE & TRAVEL
Travel – especially air travel – is a significant contributor to global climate change. At Lonely Planet, we believe that all who travel have a responsibility to limit their personal impact. As a result, we have teamed with Rough Guides and other concerned industry partners to support Climate Care, which allows people to offset the greenhouse gases they are responsible for with contributions to energy-saving projects and other climate-friendly initiatives in the developing world. Lonely Planet offsets all staff and author travel.

For more information, turn to the responsible travel pages on www.lonelyplanet.com. For details on offsetting your carbon emissions and a carbon calculator, go to www.climatecare.org.

Kilmainham & the Liberties	O'Connell St	Smithfield	Phoenix Park
Bus 10min	Walk 10min	Walk 15min	Bus 20min
Bus 15min	Walk 15min	Bus 15min	Bus 20min
Walk 15-30min	Walk 10min	Walk 10min	Bus 20min
Walk 15-30min	Walk 15min	Walk 20min	Bus 25min
n/a	LUAS 20min	LUAS 15min	LUAS 10min
LUAS 20min	n/a	LUAS 5min	LUAS 20min
LUAS 15min	LUAS 5min	n/a	LUAS 10min
LUAS 10min	LUAS 20min	LUAS 10min	n/a

into Connolly Station. Trains run from 5.30am to 12.30am every 15 minutes and every five minutes during peak times, Monday to Friday, from 6.30am on Saturday and from 7am to 11.30pm on Sunday. Fares range from €1.40 to €2.10 depending on your travel zones or an daily/weekly pass is available for €4/14. Buy tickets from machines at stops and certain newsagents.

TAXI

Taxis can be hailed on the street or found at ranks, including those at O'Connell St (Map p109, B4), College Green (Map p39, B2) and N St Stephen's Green (Map p39, B5) near Grafton St.

It can be difficult to get a taxi after pubs close Thursday to Saturday. Many companies dispatch taxis by radio but run out of cars at peak times; be sure to book

as early as you can. Try **City Cabs** (☎ 872 7272) or **National Radio Cabs** (☎ 677 2222).

Flagfall is €3.40, then €0.15 for every 200m (or 30 seconds); supplements include night travel, Sundays and bank holidays (€0.30).

PRACTICALITIES
ACCOMMODATION

If you're only in Dublin for the weekend, you'll want to stay in the city centre or a short stroll away. The addition of the LUAS tram line in 2004 has made suburban hotels more accessible so if you can't find central accommodation, that's an option worth considering. Not surprisingly, accommodation south of the Liffey is pricier than that on the northside. While some good deals can be found on the northside, most bargains are in less than

Need a place to stay? Find and book it at lonelyplanet .com. More than 55 properties are featured for Dublin – each personally visited, thoroughly reviewed and happily recommended by a Lonely Planet author. From hostels to high-end hotels, we've hunted out the places that will bring you unique and special experiences. Read independent reviews by authors and other travel aficionados like you, and get practical information including amenities, maps and photos. Then reserve your room simply and securely via Haystack – our online booking service. It's all at www.lonelyplanet.com/accommodation.

salubrious areas around Gardiner and Dorset Sts. If you stay there, keep a watch on your bags and wallets and take care when walking at night.

You can book a hotel from Ireland or abroad on **Gulliver Info Res** (www.visitdublin.com), Dublin Tourism's computerised reservations service.

DISCOUNTS

Dublin Tourism's **Dublin Pass** (1-/2-/3-/6-day €29/49/59/89) provides you with free entry to 32 attractions, free transfer on the Aircoach and 25 assorted discounts. It is available through the Dublin Tourism Centre (p174) and at the airport.

EMERGENCIES

Dublin is one of Europe's safest capitals, but pickpocketing and car break-ins are on the rise. Increased immigration has stirred racial harassment. Though they're thankfully infrequent, report serious incidents to police.

Ambulance, Fire, Police (☎ 999, 112)
Police (nonemergency) (☎ 666 6666)
Rape Crisis Line (☎ 1800 778 888)

HOLIDAYS

New Year's Day 1 January
St Patrick's Day 17 March
Good Friday March/April
Easter Monday March/April
May Day 1 May
June Holiday First Monday June
August Holiday First Monday August
October Holiday Last Monday October
Christmas Day 25 December
St Stephen's Day 26 December

INTERNET

Internet cafés are dotted all over the city, and many of then are open until late. Most public libraries offer an internet service, usually for little or no cost. If you've packed your laptop, note that the Republic uses a square-pinned, three-pronged power plug and most hotel fittings take RJ-11 phone jacks.

HOME AWAY FROM HOME

Self-catering apartments are a good option for visitors staying a few days, for groups of friends, or families with kids. Apartments range from one-room studios to two-bed flats with lounge areas, and include bathrooms and kitchenettes. Some good, central places:
Clarion Stephen's Hall (☎ 638 1111; www.premgroup.com) Deluxe studios and suites, with in-room safe, fax, modem facilities and CD players.
Home From Home Apartments (☎ 678 1100; www.yourhomefromhome.com) Deluxe one- to three-bedroom apartments in the southside city centre.
Latchfords (☎ 676 0784; www.latchfords.ie) Studios and two-bedroom flats in a Georgian town house.
Oliver St John Gogarty's Penthouse Apartments (☎ 671 1822; www.gogartys.ie)
Perched high atop the pub, these one- to three-bedroom places have views of Temple Bar.

INTERNET CAFÉS

Global Internet Café (Map p109, C5; ☎ 878 0295; 8 Lower O'Connell St; ⏲ 8am-11pm Mon-Fri, from 9am Sat, from 10am Sun)
Internet Exchange (Map p67, C3; ☎ 670 3000; 3 Cecilia St; ⏲ 8am-2am Mon-Fri, 10am-midnight Sat & Sun)

USEFUL WEBSITES

Balcony TV (www.balconytv.com)
Dublin Tourism (www.visitdublin.com)
Dubliner Magazine (www.thedubliner.ie)
Fáilte Ireland (www.ireland.travel.ie)
Irish Times (www.ireland.com)
Lonely Planet (www.lonelyplanet.com)

MONEY

In 2002, Ireland adopted the European single currency, the euro. Banks usually have the best exchange rates and lowest commission charges, though money-changers open later. Many post offices have currency exchange counters. There's a cluster of banks in College Green (Map p39, B2), opposite Trinity College, all with exchange facilities.

ORGANISED TOURS

BOAT

Liffey Voyage (Map p109, B5; ☎ 473 4082; www.liffeyvoyage.ie; Batchelor's Walk; tours €11/6; ⏲ from 11am hourly Mar-Nov) offers a historical cruise up and down the Liffey in a comfy

WI-FI HOT SPOTS

Wi-fi (or wireless fidelity) is a handy mobile alternative to plugging into a local area network (LAN). Many public places offer access to WiFi networks so that customers can use the internet on the move. Try the following hotspots for free access: Chester Beatty Library (p82), Solas (p95), Market Bar (p95), Ron Black's (p50), Globe (p94) and Aya (p46).

air-conditioned, all-weather vessel.

Be prepared to bang across the waves at up to 25 knots on **Sea Safari's** (☎ 806 1626; www.seasafari.ie; Custom House Quay; tours €30/25; ☼ from 10am, Feb-Oct) one-hour, adrenaline-pumping tours of Dublin Bay. Learn all about the Martello towers in Napoleonic times, how the Black Plague avoided Pigeon House Harbour and get a bird's-eye view into the gardens of Killiney Bay's glitterati.

Possibly Dublin's kookiest tour, **Viking Splash Tours** (Map p81, A3; ☎ 707 6000; www.vikingsplashtours.com; Bull Alley St; adult €16-18.50, child €8.95-9.50; ☼ up to 17 tours daily Feb-Nov) takes you out on a reconditioned WWII amphibious vehicle that goes to Viking sites around the city before splashing into the Grand Canal Basin for a water tour. All the while your 'craaazy' guide in Viking costume spins tales of the city.

HISTORICAL
Trinity College history graduates lead a **Historical Walking Tour** (☎ 878 0227; www.historicalinsights.ie; Trinity College; tours €12; ☼ 11am & 3pm May-Sep, 11am Apr & Oct, noon Fri-Sun Nov-Mar), a 'seminar on the street' that explores the Potato Famine, Easter Rising, Civil War and Partition. Sights include Trinity, City Hall, Dublin Castle and Four

Courts. In summer, themed tours on architecture, women in Irish history and the birth of the Irish state are also held. Tours depart from the College Green entrance (Map p39, B2).

Renowned historian author Pat Liddy and his jolly team lead **Pat Liddy's Walking Tours of Historic Dublin** (Map p109, B5; ☎ 448 7711; www.walkingtours.ie; The Liffey Voyage kiosk, Batchelor's Walk; price €10; ☼ 10.15am Mar-Nov). His informative tours cover Georgian (Monday and Friday) and Viking (Tuesday and Sunday) Dublin as well as Dublin castle and Sy Patrick's cathedral (Wednesday and Saturday) and the docklands (Thursday).

HORSE & CARRIAGE
Along the north side of St Stephen's Green (Map p54-5, C3), near Fusiliers' Arch (Map p39, B5), you can pick up a **horse & carriage** (30min around €40) for a trot around town. Most last half an hour but you can negotiate with the driver for longer trips. Carriages hold four or five people.

LITERARY & MUSICAL
The James Joyce Centre (p112) conducts one-hour walking tours of North Dublin, exploring Joyce's writings, his inspirations and various *Ulysses* landmarks. Tours depart from, and include, the centre. Book in advance.

A night tour of four literary drinking holes, the **Dublin Literary Pub Crawl** (Map p39, B4; ☎ 670 5602; www.dublinpubcrawl.com; Duke, 9 Duke St; tours €12/10; ☯ 7.30pm & noon Sun Apr-Nov, 7.30pm Thu-Sun & noon Sun Dec-Mar) is a 2¼-hour tour led by two actors who perform extracts by famous Dublin writers along the way. It's a popular tour so make a reservation ahead of time at **Dublin Tourism** (☎ 605 7700), or get to the Duke by 7pm to secure a ticket.

Two musicians play tunes and explain the evolution of Irish music in Temple Bar pubs, including the Palace Bar, Stag's Head and the Norseman, on the **Dublin Musical Pub Crawl** (Map p67, D3; ☎ 475 3313; www.discoverdublin.ie; upstairs, Oliver St John Gogarty's, cnr Fleet & Anglesea St; tours €12/10; ☯ 7.30pm May-Oct, 7.30pm Fri & Sat Nov & Feb-Apr). The professional musicians are excellent, as is the music. Be sure to arrive early to reserve your ticket.

SPOOKY

Trapeze Theatre Company runs the excellent **Ghost Walk Macabre** (☎ 087 677 1512; tour €15; ☯ 7.30pm) from Fusiliers' Arch, St Stephen's Green (Map p39, B5). It combines theatre performance with a walk through the spooky corners of Georgian Dublin. Sinister writings by Bram Stoker, Oscar Wilde and James Joyce are brilliantly drama-tised, as are some of the city's more brutal murders. Booking are essential – reserve your place the day before.

The **Zozimus Ghostly Experience** (Map p67, B4; ☎ 661 8646; www .zozimus.com; Dublin Castle gate, Dame St; tours €10/8.50; ☯ 9pm summer; 7pm winter, by arrangement) is a 1½-hour tour of Dublin's superstitious and seedy medieval past. The guide – the blind and ageing character Zozimus – recounts stories of murders, great escapes and mythical events. Bookings are essential.

PLUGS

Voltage 220V
Frequency 50Hz
Cycle AC
Plugs Flat three-pin type.

TELEPHONE
COUNTRY & CITY CODES
Ireland (☎ 353)
Dublin (☎ 01)

INTERNATIONAL DIRECT DIAL CODES
Dial ☎ 00 followed by:
Australia (☎ 61)
Canada (☎ 1)
Japan (☎ 81)
South Africa (☎ 27)
UK (☎ 44)
USA (☎ 1)

MOBILE PHONES

Ireland uses the GSM 900/1800 cellular phone system, which is compatible with European and Australian, but not North American or Japanese phones.

There are four Irish service providers: Vodafone (087), O2 (086), Meteor (085) and 3 (083). All have links with most international GSM providers, which allow you to roam onto a local service on arrival. You can also purchase a pay-as-you-go package with a local provider with your own mobile phone.

PUBLIC PHONES

Local calls from a public phone cost €0.25 for three minutes. Public phones accept coins, phonecards and/or credit cards or reverse charges.

Talk Shop (www.talkshop.ie) has several branches across the city centre, including the **Granary** (☎ 672 7212; 20 S Temple Lane; ☺ 9am-11pm) and north of the **Liffey** (Map p109, B4; ☎ 872 0200; 5 Upper O'Connell St; ☺ 9am-11pm).

USEFUL PHONE NUMBERS

Directory Inquiries (☎ 11811)
International Directory Inquiries (☎ 11818)
International Operator (☎ 114)
Ireland/Great Britain Operator (☎ 10)
Time (☎ 1191)
Weather (☎ 1550 123822)

TIPPING

Tipping is becoming more common, but is still not as prevalent as in the USA or the rest of Europe. If a restaurant adds a service charge (usually 10%) no tip is required. If not, most people tip 10% and round up taxi fares. For hotel porters €1 per bag is acceptable.

TOURIST INFORMATION

The main tourist authority is Dublin Tourism, with three walk-in-only city centre services. The **Dublin Tourism Centre** (Map p39, A3; ☎ 605 7700; www.visitdublin.ie; 2 Suffolk St; ☺ 8.30am-6.30pm Mon-Sat, 10.30am-3.30pm Sun Jul & Aug, 9am-5.30pm Mon-Sat Sep-Jun) is by far the biggest. As well as being a great source of information, the centre can book accommodation and tours. The other Dublin Tourism branches are at 14 O'Connell St (Map p109, B3) and at the Baggot St Bridge, in the foyer of **Fáilte Ireland** (☎ 1 850 230 330).

Dublin Tourism phone reservations are provided by Gulliver Info Res, a computerised service that provides up-to-date information on events, attractions and transport as well as booking accommodation. In Ireland call ☎ 1 800 668 668; in Britain ☎ 0800 668 668 66; from the rest of the world ☎ 353 669 792 083.

TRAVELLERS WITH DISABILITIES

Guesthouses, hotels and sights in Ireland are slowly being adapted for people with disabilities, but there is still a long way to go. A great deal of sights, hotels and shops are located in historic buildings that have no disabled access and cannot have lifts or ramps installed because of preservation orders.

Public transport is also problematic: some buses have low floors and designated wheelchair spots, many do not. For train travel, call ahead for an employee of **Iarnród Éireann** (Irish Rail; ☎ 703 3592; 🕐 9am-5pm Mon-Fri) to accompany you to the train and to help you off at your destination.

Wheelchair-accessible venues listed in this book appear with a ♿ symbol followed by the description 'excellent' (wheelchair access throughout the venue), 'good' (some access) and 'limited' (limited access). If in doubt, call ahead to check.

INFORMATION & ORGANISATIONS

Fáilte Ireland's annual accommodation guide, *Be Our Guest,* is available from Fáilte Ireland's larger offices and lists places that are wheelchair accessible. Obtain general information from **Comhairle** (☎ 874 7503).

Other useful organisations include the following:

Catholic Institute for the Deaf (☎ 830 0522)
Cystic Fibrosis Association of Ireland (☎ 496 2433)
Enable Ireland (Cerebral Palsy Ireland) (☎ 269 5355)
Irish Wheelchair Association (☎ 661 6183)

>INDEX

See also separate indexes for See (p180), Shop (p182), Eat (p182), Drink (p183) and Play (p184).

000 map pages

INDEX

000 map pages